Bless thee, Bottom, bless thee! Thou art translated.

Translations and Transformations

edited by Lou Rowan

Golden Handcuffs Review Publications
Seattle, Washington

Golden Handcuffs Review
Publications

Editor

Lou Rowan

Contributing Editors

Andrea Augé
Bernard Hœpffner
Stacey Levine
Rick Moody
Toby Olson
Marjorie Perloff
Jerome Rothenberg
Scott Thurston
Carol Watts

Guiding Intelligence

David Antin

LAYOUT MANAGEMENT BY PURE ENERGY PUBLISHING, SEATTLE
WWW.PUREENERGYPUB.COM

Libraries: *this is Volume II, #23.*

Information about subscriptions, donations, advertising at:
www.goldenhandcuffsreview.com

Or write to: Editor, Golden Handcuffs Review Publications
1825 NE 58th Street, Seattle, WA 98105-2440

Contents

TRANSLATION

The Masque beneath the Mask

Peter Hughes

When you're starting out as a person there are lots of words that don't mean anything except their rhythm and texture and the patterns they make with each other and with those few words, people and noises you do already know. Mum, Dad, dirty, love, kiss, goodnight etc. It's a bit disappointing when things like nursery rhymes come along so you modify them with a few rude words and the names of various kinds of imaginary fish almost without realising it. Before you know it it's time to go to school where you line up at various holes and practice sitting quietly in groups of different sizes. Soon you will be invited to write a poem about the remnants of a weasel on the nature table. Certain clues have been provided over the previous months about how the poem should be written. It's going to have a Sunday-best tone and will basically be about how the weasel can't do any weaseling any more. This poignancy has already been institutionalised, stuffed and mounted and is deeply exemplary. The tone can now be applied to cake, days, seasons, holidays, relationships, faith and youth. They don't last but they leave all this litter. Let's put some in a magazine.

One day you might want to write a poem for yourself away from institutions and the templates you have absorbed don't really fit your sense of purposelessness but you have a go anyway and your poems are like translations from your own language but maybe with some extra body parts and fish. Or they feel like someone has dug up a piece of discarded Thomas Hardy. You don't care because what you really want to do is write a pop song. Well, not so much write it as enact it in your own film which is monochrome and has a driving soundtrack and involves cigarettes, moody brunettes and sunglasses.

All poems are translations including those which enact an orgasmic exclamation or savage yelp. You're translating all the poems you ever heard into two minutes of 'your name here'. You might want to show people how wild or tidy you are and this is the birth of style. Everyone knows you're not really that wild or tidy and also no-one cares. You enact this process a few times and it gets embedded, your facility increases and it feels more natural. Editors like this and call it your distinctive voice. This is the point when many poets stop developing. But you don't want to stop here. You want to get all Picasso and try something new. You haven't, for example, had a Green Period yet (although you have been told you can't vote in the Labour leadership elections because you like the idea of solar power and clicked on something to that effect once) or made any ugly ceramics with crabs on.

We're nearly ready to make that distinction between writing a translation that helps a reader figure out what the original poem means and using an original poem as a trampoline to see over a completely different wall. Good to get that out of the way. Then we have to say that every translation, even ones that claim to be straight, are creative and interpretive acts.

My own preferred approach is to read the original and also some versions of it in Englishes. I don't want to replace any of those versions – I want to do something different. This can be refreshing for all kinds of reasons. The idea of improvising on an old tune instead of just playing the same tune again with added bongos is one we should be pretty familiar with at this stage in the history of jazz.

Anyway, when I returned to Cambridge from Italy in the early 90s Stephen Rodefer was in town and I met him after a reading he'd done, probably at the Dark Room Gallery at the top of Gwydir Street. That was a good reading space. As I recall it was a little exhibition space mainly for black and white photographs. I remember at one stage Stephen had the text of 'Four Lectures' projected on the white wall and he and his shadows moved about in front of it.

Now I'd stopped writing horrid songs for little bands I was in by the time I was about 18 so I decided to tinker with Heine and Schumann instead. Then I messed about with Paul Klee's Diaries as if I were the (moody) hero of an imagined film version set in County Clare. But one of the main effects of moving back from Italy for me was a stronger impulse to keep reading Italian, to maintain contact with that language, to keep a plate or two still spinning. I decided to read Petrarch's sonnets to see if they really were that boring. By the time I'd finished the third I knew I was going to have to regroup, adjust the lighting, put on some contemporary music and pour a stiffer drink. 317 sonnets! So now sitting more comfortably I thought I'd make some notes as I read and these turned into English 'versions' of the first couple of dozen sonnets. They were as much to do with the experience of reading this work in 21st-century Norfolk as anything else. The project gathered momentum, as things do, and I gradually settled into a stricter mode of patterning (14 lines, 10 syllables per line) partly as a nod to Wyatt and other early transformers of Petrarch in the English sonnet tradition. I found a few new and enjoyable things happening including the emergence of fresh patterns, and the reappearance of the words 'the end of the line', and also bits of pop lyric creeping in. It wasn't until I was about half-way through that I remembered Stephen Rodefer's wonderful versions of Villon and wondered just how much they had influenced my own efforts behind the scenes and whether the influence was greater than that of Roy Orbison.

So what was special about Rodefer's Villon? Here's an example.

Car Elle Sans Moy

Fuck she makes it elsewhere

all the time but I don't get
heated up behind it –
how could I?

Anyway things used to be
a whole lot worse before:
plus I'm not the stick
man I used to be.

You got to step aside sooner
or later for all those up
and coming fuckers
who gather reputation in the neighborhood

quickly enough, prized for love
and fatally hung,
making it in the aisles at church,
supple and sincere.

Rodefer shifts the setting to his own contemporary America and
employs an earthy, street tone that would not be out of place in a
Lou Reed song. He also foregrounds his own presence between the
original text and the modern reader by using a series of footnotes,
one of the greatest pleasures of this project. He seems to have
borrowed this idea from Jack Spicer's 'Heads of the Town up to the
Aether' and in Rodefer's hands the device becomes an exquisitely
wry delight. Here's one small sample.

If you try hard you can hear the sound of the earth turning.
To some it's a whirring sort of noise, to others it sounds more
like grinding. No one has been able to explain this difference
but some scientists speculate it may have something to do
with breakfast cereal.

Rodefer is not the only creative translator of classic texts of course.
Readers will have their own favourites and these might include
Blaser's Nerval, Spicer's Lorca (and Blackburn's), Tim Atkins'
Petrarch and Philip Terry's Dante. And I wouldn't want to finish these
reflections without mentioning the wonderful version of Petrarch's 'Li

Angeli eletti et l'anime beate' by John Millington Synge, who gives it an Irish lilt that might have surprised the original author.

> The first day she passed up and down through the
> Heavens, gentle and simple were left standing, and they
> in great wonder, saying one to the other:
> 'What new light is that? What new beauty at all? The like of
> herself hasn't risen up these long years from the common
> world.'
> And herself, well pleased with the Heavens, was going
> forward,
> matching herself with the most perfect that were
> before her, yet one time, and another, waiting a little, and
> turning her head back to see if myself was coming
> after her. It's for that I'm lifting up all my thoughts
> and will into the Heavens, because I do hear her praying
> that I should be making haste for ever.

When I finished my own versions of Petrarch's sonnets I started on Cavalcanti because I couldn't bear to stop. When I finished Cavalcanti I started on Leopardi for the same reason but also because I was scared of Dante and thought Leopardi was probably impossible anyway for a myriad of reasons including his back problems and general air of hopelessness. I thought Leopardi would help me quit. No, Montale, no. And everyone knows you can't mess with Pasolini.

Are we all just rewriting Petrarch anyway? Or being plainclothes troubadors amongst the shrubs in Tesco carpark. Well, no and yes and no. Of course the thing still needs to be a song even if the lute is now a stage prop made of mdf. I'm all for foregrounding the poem's participation in the various histories of song, especially since the time we all got transistor radios and generally went wireless. As for future projects I've decided to postpone my versions of Dante until at least 35 years after my death and I'm still wondering if there's time to learn German. I have a hankering to return to Heine. Is there anything finer?

from *Quite Frankly,*
after Petrarch's sonnets

Peter Hughes

105

Fiamma dal ciel su le tue treccie piova

pondering those Mussolini millions
which blacken & fatten the Vatican
I tune in to neolithic bishops
& raise a grizzled eyebrow to heaven

even the slightest internal earthquake
such as this one occasioned by breathing
turns that patch of stained-glass window into
the thinnest slip of wine-gum on her tongue

Rosie Ledet sings *Eat my Poussiere*
the smell of haddock drifts back down the street
where the merlot hums for me & my girl

in poetry meetings I guess the clerks
are talking about the death of the I
can't help it if I'm still in love with you

106

L' avara Babilonia à colmo il sacco

millionaires guffaw across the chamber
relishing another little triumph
of the people's will to be directed
by mental epidemics of the right

in the Perpendicular Gothic style
reopened by the king in October
1950 when Walter de la Mare
is publishing his *Inward Companion*

& Charles Olson airing *Projective Verse*
while religions continued to distract
us from the just & the mysterious

see the ends of all the answers streaming
out into the future night & growing
distant from our mouths & from each other

111

Quando io v' odo parlar sì dolcemente

whenever she whispers through my embers
archaic breezes from the dawn of time
revive & articulate my habit
singing silence into composition

I wonder if there's time to learn German
or paraphrase music of the future
such as Messiaen's Avignon bushes
teeming with the finches of our lady

whose hair curls back around imagined keys
to a new & unimagined music

which could lift us off the branches of time

& place which once imprisoned her presence
delicate as the egg of a goldcrest
I carry forever under my tongue

131

Or che 'l ciel e la terra e 'l vento tace

walk in local darkness hearing nothing
except the distant tinkle of the rich
the rest of us stare into burning sticks
till our eyes begin to itch & tingle

the nymph Callisto prowls the April night
shifting her weight from paw to monstrous paw
her body made of empty space & stars
paraded as a banner for all those

invisible victims of deception
twice scorned by the temporary powers
as eyesores on the edge of their estates

best to write out nights like this in charcoal
best to sing an unaccompanied song
best to speak through a mouthful of thistles

188

S' una fede amorosa, un cor non finto

if I can keep my head while all around
lovers lunge at each other's attributes
queue up for more Q8 chrysanthemums
& gift wrap inventive new vibrators

& if a face can launch a thousand ships
then why does she insist on sinking mine
not to mention her habit of snipping
through the strings of my acrobatic kite

if I were a carpenter I'd knock up
a wooden horse to park in your garden
& if I can't have you I don't want no

if I were a boy I'd do it again
I swear I wouldn't be a better man
if you're happy & you know it fuck off

291

Quel che d' odore e di color vincea

the sky smells of sodden paths through autumn
legislation arranging the wagons
into tighter & more exclusive rings
in the name of the abstract & the holy

walking is an inexpensive pastime
although the cost of fuel keeps going up
a glass of beer a bit of bread & cheese
our probe has now left the solar system

no information is available
my mind-maps are losing definition
the time has come for a good de-clutter

the time has come for running on empty
fortunately it's all downhill from here
I'm writing by the light of her dead star

from *Cavalcanty*

Peter Hughes

Cavalcanty 19

I' pregovoi che di dolor parlate

I know you've all had a lot on your minds
but I thought you might like to take a break
from your issues to concentrate on mine

which include dry rot & whistling gaskets
& an ache in the gut that's calling out
for dynarod I am these sensations
of someone else's knuckles just behind
my eyeballs which is making it tricky
to gaze reflectively upon the world
or freshen up the stale pits of my mind

& that's a shame because I'd seen some sights
& enjoyed a stunning range of inputs

which had made my mind feel like a fountain
playing incessantly throughout the nights
of a small piazza in the ghetto
instead of one of those tiny red lights
on the extension lead under the desk

I've reached that stage when glimpses of justice
& gorgeousness such as fresh leaf on beech
or any member of the cod family
proper policy her face & music
sending these little ripples through the wine
hurt my eyes & render me rickety
knowing their value & fragility

Cavalcanty 25

Posso degli occhi miei novella dire

well lookee here - it's the shock of the new
much like the schlock of the old recycled
into fresh articulations of desire

so where the fuck does all this leave us now
with our colour-coded interdental
prongs & maladjusted memory-cards
& HSBC voiceover artists
sticking fists up wooden politicians
to take the lead in steering modern art
learning health & the prospects of our love

proffer spectacular encouragement
to gargle & rock with whiskey & fire
gnaw on each of the safety-rails & chew
through every stanchion of the landing-stage
I like a salad as much as the next

panda but this time I'm engulfing trees
rafters & the roof of my own mouth

press send to flick this language through the sky
in the hope it sticks to some equipment
to which she may remember the password
& log-in details - she could read it once
then delete it forever the same way
she cancelled our multi-coloured futures
& left me with this draft in black & white

Cavalcanty 27

Donna me prega - per ch'eo voglio dire

now the lady makes me think about love's
pit-bull attacks on the soul's soft tissues
& those fatal core-reactor meltdowns
& deep immunity to metaphor
it's tricky thinking through these things in ink
as love demands we loosen up our grip
on pre-existing modes of consciousness
affiliation & self-confidence
otherwise we stand no chance of melting
flowing into fresh configurations
in response to love's accommodations
of feral power rerouted through refined
reformulations of specific lips
in actual laps tomorrow evening

so what about the inner baklava
comprising 1000s of translucent veils
crushed nuts honey dust experiences
weird terms softly brushed with olive oil &
clarified I can't believe I haven't

come yet her hair against the troubled light
trembling phone crawls right across the table
towards the rest of the rest of the world
love becomes a bustling mental impulse
with overactive elbows forever
nudging past *tutti* & barging its way
to the front of any queue or crowd
to snatch the finest view
of what's about to happen which is nothing

short of mysterious how love is made
of nothing yet feels like marble knuckles
kneading your most vulnerable hollows
articles & raw protuberances
into a species of blue slush puppy
or one of the ghostly breakdown trucks of
the apocalypse towing you at speed
the wrong way through a maze of one-way streets
by night so you can barely stay on board
that dilapidated unicycle
it's not how they portrayed it in the films
with all those unpolluted beaches or
luminous farm-free meadows without snakes
or hip umber bookshops in Manhattan

love enjoys an absence of perspective
well enjoys in the sense of despairs at
a heady blend of claustrophobia
sea-sickness & agoraphobia
are the least disagreeable symptoms
alongside earache n the genitals
dizziness & backache down the front
you keep receiving mental messages
from poets & energy companies
emergency services & phantoms
trees & insects send you final demands
the stars ask for your help with a survey
the pope calls to say if you eat those eels
you are bound to die - sorry wrong number

so love carves out an empty space which aches
to be refilled by interference waves
to vast notions in everyday persons
do what they can to keep this thing alive
through radio dedications & good
will a little card or bloom & bottle
of prosecco or on this occasion
a thoughtful Rosso di Montefalco
has moistened the tablecloth between us
& dripped on these scribbles in the notebook
lending a welcome chromaticism
to the usual black & white deceptions
which established almost every action
in our lives throughout the run-up to today

off you go young poem without dragging
a heavy tail of clever dickery
just leave without the usual excuses
drive on along anonymous ring-roads
let's stop now while the bar is still open

from *Via Leopardi*

Peter Hughes

via Leopardi 1

welcome to another roadkill idyll
& hello Britney
how you've gone downhill
since the throbbing promise
of the Beveridge Report
I don't blame you
for welling up
I mean I love this country too
& all its country musics
& the winds that blow
along the undersides
of all these desiccated leaves
& people nearly loaded stuck
stuck on admin error
switch it off unplug it
switch it on again
& where the fuck is Puck

& the Trung sisters
when you need them

via Leopardi 10

listen
an echo
of quiet
breathlessness
I breathe
you
honey
light
through
cracks
a setting
sun
for a time
the broken world
is mended
with a filigree
of molten gold

via Leopardi 13

Savlon: can I have a kiss

Vera: OK

via Leopardi 36

whenever I was young
& I was always far too young
or far too old
I hung out with a muse
who snuck me into nooks
on more than one occasion
acquainting me with the top
four or five mysteries of nature
motivational speaking & this
kind of looking over one's shoulder
posture & I asked her
how can we become more
literary & sophisticated
whilst retaining the whiff
& let's call it lustre
of a decent engine oil
but we ran out of time

A Brief Encounter

Toby Olson

Larry had managed to push out thirty-nine of the condoms, but when he got to the last one he had some trouble. He forced and grunted, and finally it broke free, plopping into the toilet bowel among the others. Each condom contained its portion of black tar heroin, and all but the one came clean in the toilet water. He lifted them out, letting that last one soak, and wiped them dry with toilet paper, then stuffed them into his pockets. The remaining one wouldn't give up its stains. It was gummy with fecal matter, and the more he wiped the stickier it got.

It was quiet in the airport men's room. Nobody in the stalls beside him, and he heard only what he thought was two men at the urinals, a cough and a groan. So he decided to head out to one of the sinks, where there was soap.

"What ya got there?" an old man two sinks down called out. The place had quickly filled, probably some plane had arrived. All the urinals were in use, and men were going into the stalls to piss.

Larry mumbled something as he soaped up the condom, then heard a shuffling of feet behind him.

"Looks like drugs to me. You one a them coyotes they talk about?"

He turned and saw five or six men, shoulder to shoulder, looking into his sink.

"Not coyotes, man," a tall, tough looking guy in the back of the growing gathering called out. "Coyotes are people smugglers. These guys are called mules. Then use balloons or condoms. Right up the ass. You a mule?"

Larry had finished washing the condom, and when he turned to head to the towel dispenser to dry it, he saw that the crowd had tightened and was looking at him suspiciously.

Quick thinker that he was, he held up the condom and waved it at the gathering.
"This," he said, "is not a balloon or a condom. This is a colostomy bag." He held it out and shook it. "And what's inside here is my shit." He glared at them, forcing them back just a little.

"My mother had one of those," a man a few sinks down called out.

"Mine too, but it was a hell of a lot bigger than *that* ."

Larry addressed that man, a short fellow, maybe forty, going bald.

"They come in various sizes," he said, "depending on the medical issues. Okay? Now that y'all have violated my privacy, God Dammit!, back off!"

"Let's see it," somebody said.

"See what?" Larry answered, his voice full of anger.

"That hole place were you slip in on."

There was no hole of course, and Larry thought to brazen it out. But now he saw that the men, though still suspicious, were curious as well, and he had to come up with something else.

"The hole closes when the bag is detached for washing."

"It never did on my mother."

"Mine either."

"This is new," Larry said. "A new medical technique. Now if your finished with your questions, you can step aside."

Not one of them did.

"Okay, okay. You wanna see it? Okay, for God's sake!"

He turned back to the sink, unbuttoned his shirt, and worked the gum he'd been chewing out of his mouth and into his hand. Then he hunched over and opened the condom and tried to connect it. He found a way, then turned and faced the gathering. Using the gum he had attached the condom to his right nipple. It hung there, the weight of the black tar heroin causing it to sway.

"Good God!" one of them said. "That's your nipple!"

"Yes, it would seem so," Larry answered. "But this is the route the intestine takes to get to the surface."

"Why da ya say 'root' instead of 'rout'? Ain't that from a tree, some bushes?"

"Because my pronunciation is correct, that's why. Your pronunciation of 'root' as 'rout' has the word referring to a successful storming of a castle, a Chicago Bears game in which that team has lost by forty points or more, not a direction between places. Route is properly pronounced 'root.' Hey, I hope there aren't any Bears fans in here!"

The men laughed and punched each other on the shoulders.

"What about the nipple?" somebody said.

"Boy, do I like a good discussion."

"Oh yeah, me too."

He gazed down at his nipple and the swaying condom full heroin. Then he looked up at them and spoke.

"Three years ago, the Mayo clinic in Minnesota began a secret series of tests, using cadavers, to try to invent some new ways with bowel resections, one that would account for the differences between people. And people *are* different when it comes to their vital insides. Their discoveries bore fruit, and my operation was the product, an application of science to real life

"What looks like a nipple to you is really a doorway to a tunnel, one that expels and renders half of the fecal matter into a liquid form. You see how it's attached? The nipple itself is really a miniaturized pump. It drawn the liquid parts of the fecal matter into the bag. What's in *this* bag -he caressed the hanging condom- is part of the other half of the fecal deposit, that which remains firm."

"My Lord, a medical breakthrough," said an awestruck voice.

"You can say that again."

"I'll sure as hell remember this for a long time."

"What's your handle, stranger?" A young man said in a cowboy twang.

All the men laughed and punched each other on the shoulders.

"It's Jessie, just Jessie."

"That's a corker!"

"Now, would you please get the hell out of my way? It's time I rode out."

Larry was buttoning up as he stepped forward, and some caught a glimpse of the oscillating condom before the shirt, that was a curtain, hid it from view.

They part like the Red Sea, he thought, and soon he was out of the terminal and on the sidewalk in the sun.

He stood there smiling for a few moments. He could feel the smooth surface of the condom traveling through the hair on his chest.

"I think I'll wear it for a while," he said out loud, then walked away.

Plastic Surgery

Toby Olson

The first time he saw Natasha, he was taken by her tall, statuesque figure and her Russian beauty. She had been a model (well, she still was then), and he found her awkward English and their brief conversation quite charming. They had met at a gallery opening, a strange and compelling showing of enhanced photographs of women's faces, and though he admired the faces of women, he found that he was unmoved by these depictions.

He was a salesman for Barrett and Johnson insurance company, indeed the Salesman of the Year (1983), and he was out on the town, still basking in the glory of that honor. Once they had spoken their few words, she was swallowed up by a crowd of admirers, and he had left and gone to a bar, in which he sat on a stool, a whisky close at hand, and thought about her and the inheritance he had just received, five million dollars from his cousin's uncle on the mother's side. He'd never met the man and had no idea as to why he'd become the recipient of such wealth. His name was Norman.

And so it was that they met again, in a park beside a giant maple tree encircled by a bench, the boards of which were dappled by sunlight and warmed and cushioned their bodies as they leaned

back against them, sweet scent of the tree's bark and the twitter
of sparrows invisible among the branches and leaves above. The
faint, cheerful voices of children in the distance and the gurgle of
a fountain provided background music for their casual talk, softly
punctuating the cool stillness of the day.

And that was it. A dozen or so dates, dinner and movies, six
months, and they were married.

And things were just fine in the beginning. In their new
life, they spoke often, but briefly, and very entertainingly. She was
a wonderful cook, preparing, with great fanfare, various Russian
dishes. She wore her model clothing around the apartment, a
condominium that he had purchased a few years before, and he
often noticed her posing before large mirrors, ones she had brought
with her into their marriage. She had brought other things as well,
expensive modern furniture, fancy lamps, bed linens. She'd pushed
his utilitarian stuff aside or had gotten rid of it. He didn't mind these
losses, nor the ones having to do with his clothing. She dressed
him in designer stuff, up from shorts and jeans all the way to a tux
for fancy parties, the ones they never attended now that she was
struggling with her career.

Then she had plastic surgery. She'd said she needed it in
order to get those now illusive modeling jobs. He understood this,
and he was fine with it, noticing no changes of expression when
she came home, hid in her room, then appeared one day in her new
face. They were both forty-three years old. The jobs were few and far
between, and she grew increasingly frustrated and angry about that.
For some reason, angry at him as well.

*For expecting it of me to cook only!? Lookit at me, this face!
Still is beautiful? Why no jobs then? It is you I think. Holding me
preventing. All times stupid! I say, lookit at me!*

But he was not looking at her. He sat at his neat desk most
evening, studying actuarial tables, settling claims, examining his new
investments. And so her anger increased. He was five foot seven,
and she would bang into his stomach with her hip, then stride off, as
if she were moving down some fashion week runway. Occasionally
she wacked him on the back of his head with her open palm or
a wooden spoon. She worked out, pilates, weights, miles on her
stationary bike. She was six foot three, and that in her stocking feet.

Norman had often wondered about plastic surgery,

especially that designed to improve the faces of women. It was never some returning, going back to a time when one was younger, though that seemed most often to be the intent. What was it then?

He was thinking these things on his three mile walk, heading back home from the office, his only exercise, which he accomplished at a good pace, though on this day he could be seen limping slightly, from behind, his bowed legs more prominent that usual. He had felt blood on the back of his left knee upon awaking. She had leaned down and stabbed him there when he had approached too close while she was filleting the striped bass last night. *Get away you!* she had yelled at him. He thought she might have interfered with some tendon or ligament back there. The wound was quite painful.

But these women, he was thinking. In some of the worse cases and some of the better ones too, he had seen a sheen, a glowing of the skin that made it seem as if a thin sheet of polyester film had been tightly affixed there to provide a certain youthfulness that though apparent at a distance was no more than a subtle covering of the actual on closer examination. Some of the women seemed to know this as a bit of fakery and would look away. But this was perception only, Norman understood, a metaphor, and he knew the reality was quite different from that.

Walking. His leg aching. Limping. The small rise of the hump on his back more prominent as he motored slowly along. His natural tonsure, his scalp glistening with sweat. Two more miles. What was it that Natasha had seen in him? What did he see in her?

He knew that their marriage was nearing its final stage, that he no longer loved her, nor she him. In the beginning, and for a long while, it had been her beauty, her stature and presence. For her, he thought, it had been his money, then his honor, Salesman of the Year after all, though she had seemed a bit jealous at his success. She wasn't working, hadn't been for a long while now. Though she was still beautiful, she was too old, and the plastic surgery hadn't helped. She was enraged all the time now, and the brutality she inflicted upon him was, in reality, an attack on her own body. She felt she was falling apart and wished only that he would join her. These were deep understandings, as he trundled along, thinking of his leg and the ways in which he seemed to be losing the structures of his life.

He'd always been a man who valued order, both in his

doings and in his person, but recently his client lists had fallen into a shambles. He was no longer out on the road visiting prospects, something other high level executives at Barrett and Johnson had never done. He'd been thought of as a wonder salesman, someone who stayed close to his clients, got down in the dirt with them. Kindly, yet shrewd, he managed to set records in lowering payoffs that otherwise might have been astronomical.

And then there was his dress and grooming. He'd stopped shaving every day, and would appear at work with a shadow of hair on his face. Some thought it was a style matter, the scruffy look, yet most were aware of some difficulty. His unkempt fringe of hair, his soiled and wrinkled clothing. Often he worked at home, in his study, and didn't make it to work at all. The top boss was watching him, cognizant of the facts and that he might be in serious trouble. Salesman of the Year was well behind him now. It no longer carried much weight.

He was passing a row of stores now in his slow perambulation, a gourmet food shop, its delectable wares, cheeses and prepared dishes, on shelves facing the window; a fancy fish store; a gift shop, various greeting cards, glass paper weights, display cases full of expensive soaps garishly packaged, tumblers, small ceramic frogs; and at the end of the row, a women's clothing boutique.

He paused, his knee was aching, and he was tired. And through the large plate glass window he spied a women who stood out from the other customers and elegantly dressed sales staff. She was tall and slim and wore a fine linen sheath dress and had moved to a floor length free standing mirror that faced away from the window outside of which Norman stood. She was facing him, examining herself, and he could see her clearly. Perhaps forty year old, he thought, beautiful, and she had been touched by the surgeon's knife.

He had seen many women who'd had their faces professionally carved, and even looking at this one, whose operation had been of a very high quality and was for the most part invisible, he could tell that work had been done. He could see it in a tightness at the edge of her eye, an elevation of her cheeks, and the way she lifted her chin in order to display, even to herself now, her new neck.

Now he saw clearly what he had imagined he'd seen before.

The warm voices and graceful gestures of such women were the same as they had been, though somewhat aggressive now, or mildly strident. Often they seemed subtly ventriloquised. When they spoke their words might be sweet or angry or simply fed up, but they floated on a soft red slide, which was the tongue, and their deliverance was fragrant and of cold, hard thinking and of deep understanding. This even while yelling.

And then he saw what he knew was the most important things: the eyes and the two faces. She was there in the window, and she saw him and she looked at him. Maybe it was his injury or his exhaustion. Maybe it was the coolness of the early fall day. Her eyes blinked once, then stared at him. And in their deep blue pools, hardly perceptible at first, he could see through to the other eye. He lowered his gaze to her face, and there, in it or through it or behind it, he saw the other, deeper face. The surface was a thin, beautiful, mask, and the vaguely seen, though strong and relaxed presence behind it was who she was, or not quite, for it was she who had wanted this improvement and was now both the mask and the spirit.

He felt he could speak to her, imagined that he had, and the more he looked and looked, the image of the one he was speaking to came forward and the mask became just that, something to see through. He'd been speaking to, and was now looking at, the spirit behind the mask, the controller. There came a moment in their reverse movements when the two faces came together. And there was the beautiful, fully integrated, woman. Then the two faces separated and the spirit took over again.

"I shoulda got the fuckin money. He was my uncle, not yours!"

He turned, and there was his cousin Fred, that bulky guy, a weightlifter who dabbled in cage fighting. And Norman could see that he was back on steroids once again. He was almost vibrating. He said nothing more, then lunged at him and began punching him in the face and body. It hurt like hell, and even though Fred came to his senses quickly, the damage had been done. A crushed cheek bone, a fracture of the patella on the opposite side of his damaged leg, his nose broken and pushed dramatically to the side.

And so it was that he was staggering up the stairs to his apartment on the second floor. He'd tried to wipe the blood away with his shirt, but it had coagulated and was sticky and close to impossible to rub off. He reached the landing, then opened the door and entered into the living room, only to find her once again examining herself in one of her mirrors. She glimpsed his reflection to the side of her shoulder and turned.

My Got! What is happening to you? You are one big mess!

Her words were delivered out of kindness, he thought. But as she approached, a look of concern upon her face, he saw what he had seen in the shop window, the mask, and below it the character of the controller. She was there, the real Natasha, that face and those eyes that she had manipulated so successfully in the time of their marriage before plastic surgery. Now the manipulation was on the surface, and her real face had relaxed into the person she really was. It was a face of pure evil. He saw it in her burning eyes, in the blood rising in her cheeks.

She crossed the room, staring at him, smiling now, and reached down and lifted him up into her arms. Then she moved to the closed window, paused, and threw him into the glass.

They were only on the second floor, and he landed in a dumpster full of garbage bags that cushioned his fall. He was lucky to get away with only a cracked hip and a broken ankle, and these added to his other injuries made it necessary that an ambulance be called. His downstairs neighbor took care of this. Natasha was nowhere to be seen.

He was in the hospital close to a month, and his cousin Fred, still profusely apologetic about the beating, sat by his bedside every day as he recovered, and when he left the hospital, it was Fred who drove him to the studio apartment that he had arranged for.

It was a small, but nice enough place, and Fred went to the apartment with a rental truck and gathered what was left of Norman's furniture.

"She didn't say a thing. Not anything. What happened?"

And Norman told him the story that he had told the police. He had stumbled and his bum leg has given out and he had crashed through the window.

Fred was suspicious, as the police had been, but Norman stuck to the story, and in the end his version of the event was accepted.

He got a lawyer, then he contacted a plastic surgeon, and before long he had a new face, was back at work, and had organized his affairs. He settled one million dollars on Fred. Natasha received two million and the apartment, and he was left with what remained, enough for a new condominium, a two bedroom in a high rise closer to work, and anything he might desire, a car, clothing, travel. He desired very little, just his work, a fine single malt Scotch, a little TV, and a good book for bedtime reading.

He knew the two faces were there now, but he never spent time before mirrors, and in a while he figured that the two had fused together, the controller had come to the surface.

And so it was that others began to noticed the openness of his new expression. They saw it as welcoming, in no way dissembling, and sincere. He acquired new friends, went dancing with a small graceful woman, vacationed in Cabo San Lucas. His smile was contagious. He became light on his feet.

He has seen me from behind my face, so out window. Crack hip, broking ankle. Not much.

This man Norman husband was fool. I put up all years! Some time I had wish for sledgit hammer!

Yes, was money. Now I have. Two million coming from uncle of cousin on other side.

I have it my house, my beemer, my model stuff clothings, my best furnitures. I have it not stupid fuck Norman.

I have it also my mirrors.

There I am now. Lookit at me.

I am so pretty!

Theocritus: Rough, Rougher, Roughest Trades and Commentary

George Economou

The Greek Anthology 9. 338

Εὕδεις φυλλοστρῶτι πέδῳ, Δάφνι, σῶμα κεκμακός
  ἀμπαύων, στάλικες δ' ἀρτιπαγεῖς ἀν' ὄρη·
ἀγρεύει δέ τυ Πὰν καὶ ὁ τὸν κροκόεντα Πρίηπος
  κισσὸν ἐφ' ἱμερτῷ κρατὶ καθαπτόμενος,
ἄντρον ἔσω στείχοντες ὁμόρροθοι. ἀλλὰ τὺ φεῦγε,   5
  φεῦγε μεθεὶς ὕπνου κῶμα † καταγρόμενον.

Rough Trade

Daphnis, you sleep on a bed of leaves on the ground to give
  your weary body a break after staking your nets in the hills;
but Pan's on the hunt for you and Priapus adorns
  his head by crowning it with crocus and ivy,
the two approaching your cave in concert. So run,
  run, slip out of the deep sleep that makes you their prey.

Rougher Trade

Sleepy-head hunter, now you're the hunted,
with Pan and Priapus hot on your t(r)ail.
Better split before they steal into your cave,
split, Daphnis, before they commence ramming.

Roughest Trade

... the peter of Pan
                           stiff as a shoot
for the herdsboy
                           eluding
his lusty
           pursuit
intact and in perfect
                           suspension
as by the painter shown
as by the poet sung ...

Commentary

Late in 2010, I responded to an invitation from the editor of
Asymptote with a translation in three parts entitled "Rough
Trade" of a fragment surviving in a Cologne papyrus from the
second century AD by the ancient Greek poet Archilochus
(fl. 648 BC). It was published in the January 2011 issue and
subsequently reprinted in my book *Unfinished and Uncollected*
(Shearsman Books, 2015, p. 97):

Gone's the bloom from your soft skin, your furrow's
withered too, the ... of foul old age is taking its toll,
          ] and the sweet loveliness has bolted from your
     longed for face.
          ] for already many blasts of wintry winds
have assailed you, and many, many times ...

(rougher trade)

Now that Mother Nature's done her bit,
rewrapping you in sags and wrinkles,
sprinkling your pussy with salt and pepper,
your elective surgeries finish the job
with that blinkless freeze-dried face.

(roughest trade)

Once your looks were out-of-sight
but now they ought to be again.

Beginning with the idea that translating a poem involves
a process that we should concede constitutes a kind of
rough trade between poets, their languages and cultures,
I proceeded to compose a rendition that to the best of my
abilities and intentions presents an accurate, approximate
version of one of Archilochus' contributions to a long standing
popular theme in ancient Greek lyric: a lover–poet's gleeful
expression of the revenge of time upon the beauty of a former
non-reciprocating object of his affection. Shortly thereafter, I
was inspired to write two more versions that would be directed
by the comparative and superlative degrees of "rough." Though
the fragmentary state of the original may have played a role in
my decision to try this, my primary goal was not so much to
come up with a complete translation of a text partially violated
by time and accident as it was to dig more deeply into my
encounter with the Archilochian text in order to challenge
myself to seek new possibilities for translating a poem in a
series of stages. The levels of "rougher" and "roughest" were
conceived and executed with the intention of exploring new
and unexpected contexts and textures for the poem rather than
by a wish to produce a more finished adaptation or do-over of
the level of "rough."
          Although I often thought of pursuing further attempts
in this approach to poetic translation, it took another editorial
invitation a few years later from Lou Rowan to contribute to this
special "Bless thee, Bottom, bless thee! Thou art translated"

issue of *Golden Handcuffs Review* to get me thinking about a return to the experiment. During a recent rereading of Theocritus (fl. early third century BC), recognized as the inventor of bucolic/ pastoral poetry, I came across a much-admired epigram of his preserved in the renowned *Greek Anthology.* Unlike his much longer and complex *Idylls*, such a short, intense poem, which evokes the pastoral tradition, its mountainous setting, and its singular *erotico rusticano*, struck me as especially suitable for a next try at rough trade translating. The result, which appears at the beginning of this piece, follows the general lines of approach developed in the working out of the three-part Archilochus fragment, though it does not attempt to duplicate its outcomes. The "rough-rougher-roughest" paradigm, in other words, serves not as a boilerplate but as a flexible itinerary.

For the rough trade version of the action-packed fast moving epigram, which was written in elegiac couplets (alternating dactylic hexameters and pentameters of quantitative verse), I tried to match my lines to the original's as much as possible, combining as many iambic and dactylic feet in them as I could to produce a lively rhythm. For the three principals in the poem, Daphnis, Pan, and Priapus, one should consult the articles on them in any one of the many available reference books on classical mythology. But I would point out that Daphnis and Pan appear often and play important roles in the *Idylls of Theocritus.* Daphnis, a Sicilian cowherd who became a major figure in the pastoral tradition, was a beautiful, brilliant young poet and musician whose mysterious and tragic death by drowning contributed to the rise of bucolic poetry when he passed his pipes on to Pan before he died. Though he was beloved by the Muses and the Nymphs of the forest, Daphnis was deeply conflicted, and his fate has been described as enacting "a tragic union between art and death."[1] Pan, a son of Hermes, was the part goat and part human god of flocks and pastures first worshipped in Arcadia; a fertility god as well, he was endowed with great sexual energy, which he directed––or rather directed him––with indiscriminate ardor

---

[1]Charles Segal, *Poetry and Myth in Ancient Pastoral: Essays on Theocritus and Virgil,* Princeton University Press, 1981, p. 27.

towards all available targets. Priapus, the son of Aphrodite and Dionysus, was also a fertility god and a guardian of orchards and gardens, a puny scarecrow figure of a man sporting a monstrously enormous erect penis. He, or at least his name, lives on today in the condition called "priapic." Two final issues concerning the writing of this first version arose in the closing couplet of the epigram. At the end of verse five and the beginning of verse six, Theocritus uses the same word, φεῦγε (literally *flee, get away*), which I translated as "run" and whose sequence in the lines I kept in order to retain the urgency of their imperative force achieved through his use of *anadiplosis*, a rhetorical device used in the construction of repetitions that entails the linking of two phrases, clauses, or verses by repeating the word at the end of the first one at the beginning of the one that follows. And finally, the last word in the last line, καταγρόμενον, from a verb meaning *to catch, capture, to overtake*, though marked as dubious in the text, has not been convincingly replaced by any editorial conjecture. I have retained it as the word on which to base my translation, not only out of necessity but also out of a sense that it may well be the right word, given the image of the hunt established by the first word in line three and the derivational paradigm to which both words belong.

Like its counterpart rougher version of the Archilochus fragment, this one introduces synopsis to the action and a more contemporary idiom to its diction. Even the exhortation to leave the premises abandons the more formal rhetorical device of *anadiplosis* for a more conversational parallelism that is darkened by its slangy imperative choice of to "split" with its associative hint of what could happen to Daphnis if he fails to get out of the cave in time. These choices, along with the typographically designed wordplay "t(r)ail," contribute to the compacted, speeded-up account of the narrative and tend to create some distance between this version and the preceding one; nevertheless, "rough" and "rougher" remain recognizably connected. The poet-translator of "rougher," though definitely acting more on his own than he is in "rough," is still translating Theocritus' poem. But in both the Archilochus and the Theocritus "roughest" stages, there is an appearance of the disappearance of the translator altogether, which is the result of the shifting sequential nature of the poet-translator's involvement with the text. His work as translator begins to gear down as he moves from the first to the second stage just as his work as poet begins to gear up, a process that becomes complete in the third and final stage. Removed from their original contexts, each of these final versions could hypothetically be read as separate poems.

But to keep it in context, the last phase of this sequence comes across more like an analogue than a redaction and appears to have dropped into our laps like an anonymous poetic fragment or a shard of pottery from the antique past even though the wording of its synecdochic presentation of Pan, pulling in the opposite chronological direction, may well remind us of his modern descendant, J. M. Barrie's flute-playing, leafy-costumed "boy who wouldn't grow up." The suspended erotic chase as depicted in this stop-watched version at best barely reflects the inconclusive ending of the original poem and its rough trade version, both of which close on an unresolved note of a lecherous assault and a need to escape it. The rapid, urgent accounts of the action in "rough" and its sequel "rougher," though they conclude somewhat ambiguously, still seem to be open to the taking of bets. Not so in the "roughest." There the scene is absolutely static, duplicating the one created by the mid-fifth century BC Pan-painter in his famous red-figure name vase, on one side of which "The goat-god Pan, with human body, billy-goat's head, feet and tail, extends human hands towards the young goatherd, wearing a wooly cap, animal skin over his tunic, and boots. With 'choreographed' steps they glide past a woodland herm on a rock."[2] Possibly out of a sense of propriety, the writer of this description omits to mention the two erections in the picture: the first one, the "peter of Pan/ stiff as a shoot," and the second, the abnormally long upstanding one on the woodland herm, whose image we immediately recognize as none other than Priapus. The appearance of Pan's fellow hunter of Daphnis in the epigram by Theocritus

---

[2]Database, the Beazley Archive, Classical Art Research Centre, University of Oxford. The vase belongs to the Boston Museum of Art collection.

is symbolic rather than dynamic here, and his presence, reduced in importance, is not as evidently active as it is in the poem––a modified instance of *ut pictura poesis*. Because the supportive role of Priapus in this forever frozen configuration of "lineaments of [un]gratified desire" in the vase painting constitutes a notable alteration and diminution of this god's participation in the erotic pursuit, I decided to go with that flow and edit him out as a literal player in the action of my ironically fragmented final and most independent representation of Theocritus' poem. There is room enough for him to stand up in the countryside for his amorous motives in many of the works that the painters and poets of old show and sing.[3]

---

[3]In another of Theocritus' epigrams in *The Greek Anthology* (9.437), the speaker urges a goatherd to seek out and pray in his behalf to the "gracious god Priapus," a recently carved statue out of a fig tree without legs or ears and covered with bark but still equipped with a potent tool with which to do the works of Aphrodite. It is three times as long, the epigram, that is, as the typical ones in the anthology and full of conventional motifs such as the *locus amoenus* set piece. Wittily driven to an unexpected conclusion, its Priapus just stands still in the lovely woods and listens.

Ethical Criticism and the Challenges Posed by Innovative Poetry

Hank Lazer

Introduction

My essay "Ethical Criticism and the Challenges Posed by Innovative Poetry" is an expanded version of a keynote address that I delivered on November 29, 2015 in Jinan, China, at the 4th Convention of the Chinese/American Association for Poetry and Poetics. For this essay to make (some) sense to an American audience, there are contexts that require some explanation. Ethical Criticism is a literary critical movement in contemporary Chinese academia, particularly in the area known as the study of Foreign Literatures. Once again, due to governmental pressures (in China), it has become necessary to justify the value of studying Western literature, including contemporary American literature (particularly more innovative writing). Once again, professors in China may need to justify such courses and related research and writing. Professor Nie (Central China Normal University – CCNU) has emerged as an articulate spokesperson and theoretician for what has become known as "ethical criticism" – a movement not without criticism and (often subdued) critique within Chinese academic circles. However, the advocacy of "ethical criticism" (in China) also represents a politically astute defense of the value of engaging a range of Western literatures. Thus the emergence of "ethical criticism" has a radically different cultural, political, and institutional meaning in China than such a development would have in the US. Truly, the situation for Chinese academics is more nuanced and complex than my brief introduction can explain. My talk represents a critique of the limited range (and obsessive practicality and reductiveness) of the initial development of "ethical criticism." Indeed, the speaker (a well-published senior professor from Peking University) whose talk immediately followed mine presented an old guard defense of classical Western literature and a direct attack on the "immorality" and "unnaturalness" of much contemporary American writing. To my surprise and great pleasure, Professor Nie welcomed my talk and immediately promised to publish the essay in two of China's leading journals – *Foreign Literature Studies* (April 2016 – 38.2: 7-20 and *Forum for World Literature Studies* (March 2016-8.1: 1-18). The other risky (and perhaps foolish) aspect of my talk involves speaking to a Chinese audience about the value of a careful (and ethical) reading of Lao Tzu's *Tao Te Ching*. (Think coals to Newcastle..?) I have been studying the *Tao Te Ching* for the past fifteen years (and consult numerous translations and commentaries); I have been teaching the Tao Te Ching for several years in an undergraduate seminar in Zen Buddhism and Radical Approaches to the Arts. To my surprise, I learned that Chinese college students had at best a vague awareness of the *Tao Te Ching*, and few literature/foreign literature professors had any substantive engagement with the text. My remarks initiated some very exciting conversations (and gave me a sense that Chinese readers would soon be returning to a more sustained reading of Lao Tzu's great poem).

***

When good is near you, when you have life in yourself, it is not by any known or accustomed way; you shall not discern the footprints of any other; you shall not see the face of man; you shall not hear any name; —the way, the thought, the good, shall be wholly strange and new.
– Emerson, *Self-Reliance* (158)

Thus far, ethical criticism has applied perspectives, questions, concepts, and historical and cultural contexts primarily to the study of works of fiction and drama. I wish to begin by saluting Professor Nie for his internationally noteworthy and celebrated development of this field of study![i] (And I am honored that he has written a Preface for the Chinese translation of my Selected Poems.[ii]) I wish to expand the range of consideration in ethical criticism, principally through an investigation of some ways that such criticism might proceed with regard to modern and contemporary poetry, and most especially with regard to innovative contemporary poetry.

If we begin by setting the groundwork for an ethical criticism, we must do so by attending to the nature of the activity as established by Professor Nie. As noted in a recent article in *The Times Literary Supplement* ("Fruitful Collaborations: ethical literary criticism in Chinese academe," by William Baker and Shang Biwu, 29 July 2015) – which in and of itself is an indication of the international importance of Professor Nie's work – ethical criticism refers to

> an approach that reads, analyzes and interprets literature from an ethical perspective. It takes literary texts as its very object of analysis, and aims to shed a new light on a variety of relationships depicted by literature such as man/woman and him/herself, humans and others, humans and nature, and humans and society, from an ethical perspective. (14)

Baker and Shang in the TLS article go on to summarize:

> Specifically, ethical literary criticism embraces the following five aspects: (1) it investigates the moral values of writers and their historical backgrounds and the connections between writers' own moral values and those ethical values projected in their creative output; (2) it investigates the relations between moral phenomena existing in a writer's work and in reality, the moral inclinations, and the social and moral values of that work; (3) it examines the effects of that work's moral values as exerted on readers and society, and readers' evaluations of the moral thoughts of writers and their works; (4) it evaluates the influence of writers'

and theirs works' moral inclinations on other contemporary writers and literature; and (5) it uncovers the moral features of writers and their works and aims to explore various issues concerning the relations between literature and society or literature and writer from an ethical perspective. (14)

My talk today really represents a development and expansion of that fifth area of ethical criticism. And my remarks may be seen as a continuation of those made by my good friend Charles Bernstein in his talk at the 3rd CAAP conference, "Pitch of Poetry" (which appears in *Forum for World Literature Studies*, Vol. 7, No. 3 September 2015, pp. 426-438), specifically Charles' sense of poetics and poetic practice as dialogical and his contrasting of ethics with morality wherein "poetics cannot claim the high ground of morality or systematic theory" (427). As Charles develops his perspective in "Pitch of Poetry," poetry involves an ethics of non-utility and is participatory in art-making without ulterior purpose. Most interesting of all, since Charles is rarely thought of as a "spiritual" poet, his perspective in "Pitch of Poetry" is remarkably consonant with Lao Tzu's ethics in the *Dao de jing* (an ethics that I will return to later and contrast somewhat with the ethics of Lao Tzu's contemporary, Confucius):

> Poetry makes *nothing* happen ..., manifest in the cracks (delays, blanks) between words and the frictions of gift. A gift (this gift) is a present made present; as for reciprocity: nothing is given in return.
> Mine is a homely poetics, both odd-looking (unattractive, disagreeable, low) and intimate (even private). (435)

*

Ethical criticism is important for (at least) two reasons: (1) it is a Chinese theory of literary criticism, and thus it alters, challenges, and enlivens (from a very particular cultural and historical perspective) the range of international conversations and writings about literature and the value of literary study (at a time, perhaps, when the practicality of literary study is being treated by the public and by university planners and administrators somewhat skeptically);

and (2) it inevitably returns us to a fundamental set of questions (often bypassed as our critical considerations become more "sophisticated" and specialized and professionalized?) about *why we read*, and about the value of studying literature and reading literature (particularly so-called difficult literature) intensely and carefully.

*

When I gave a keynote address at the 2nd CAAP conference, in Wuhan, I advocated the study of two 20th century American poets who were, I felt, under-represented in Chinese considerations of American poetry: George Oppen and Larry Eigner. That address – subsequently published in Foreign Literature Studies (Wuhan, China), Vol. 35, No. 5 (October 2013): 9-22 as "The Peculiarities of the Making of Cross-Cultural Literary History: Poetry of George Oppen and Larry Eigner,"– might also, retrospectively, be considered as a type of ethical criticism, asking the question what else needs to be included in an emerging Chinese version of American Literary History, particularly in the domain of modern and contemporary poetry. For there is an ethics that pertains to which poetry is, through textbooks, anthologies, translations, official literary histories, and syllabi, allowed or likely to be read. I am pleased to report that in the past couple of years, the situation with regard to Oppen in China is changing somewhat, as Xiaosheng Yang's translation of Oppen's most important long poem, "Of Being Numerous," has been published in China.[iii]

Oppen's poetry still does provide an extremely interesting and provocative instance of how ethical criticism might establish its relationship to modern American poetry. One might begin by considering Oppen's work from a biographical perspective – just as one engages the choices made by characters in works of fiction and drama, thinking about the historical circumstances of choices that Oppen made as poet and person, most especially his affiliation with the Communist Party – an affiliation that obviously has a radically different meaning in America than in China! – which necessitated his leaving America to live for a substantial period of time in Mexico. Oppen was only able to return to the US once the McCarthy Era persecution of Communists ceased in the late

1950s. One might also reflect on Oppen's decision to remain silent as a poet for twenty-five years. Or, one might think about a less well known refusal that Oppen made. Once he returned to writing and publishing poetry, Oppen's work eventually did receive recognition. In 1969 he was awarded the Pulitzer Prize for his book *Of Being Numerous*. While most poets choose to cash in on such success – developing reading tours and speaking engagements (with significantly enhanced fees due to the receipt of this prestigious national prize) – Oppen chose to cancel a developing reading tour, preferring to work on his writing.

If we turn to Oppen's poetry itself, while there are many locations for contemplation of the ethical dimensions raised by the poems, I would simply point to two particular instances. First, in "Of Being Numerous" one of Oppen's central considerations is the dialectical and complex relationship between singular and collective identity. After noting the shipwreck and subsequent "rescue" of Robinson Crusoe, Oppen writes,

> Obsessed, bewildered
>
> By the shipwreck
> Of the singular
>
> We have chosen the meaning
> Of being numerous. (section 7, OBN)

And just as Mao in China gave ongoing consideration to the ideal relationship of intellectuals and artists to the people, Oppen too wonders and faces the distinct possibility that "'Whether, as the intensity of seeing increases, one's distance from Them, the people, does not also increase'" (section 9, OBN),[iv] causing Oppen to wonder as well "if to know is noble" (section 31, OBN). It is this complex and unflinchingly honest consideration of how to honor simultaneously one's singularity and one's commitment to a human collective that runs throughout Oppen's poetry.

Second, in "Till Other Voices Wake Us," the last poem in *Primitive* (1978), Oppen's last published book, the concluding lines are a small but crucial revision of some very famous lines from T. S. Eliot's "The Love Song of J. Alfred Prufrock," a revision which is absolutely essential to understanding how Oppen's ethics differs radically from modernists such as Pound and Eliot. In Oppen's poem, Eliot's alienation and fear of engagement with humanity–"Till human voices wake us, and we drown" – becomes "till other voices wake/ us or we drown" (p. 286, *New Collected Poems*). For Oppen, the voices of other human beings, far from being something threatening that might drown us, are precisely that which rescues and awakens us. One other noteworthy revision by Oppen is of Shelley's classically romantic and fabulously grandiose notion that "poets are the unacknowledged legislators of the world," which, in Oppen's hands becomes, in the poem "Disasters," "legislators// of the unacknowledged// world" (267). It is that unacknowledged world that I will return to later in this talk, particularly as I consider the *Dao de jing*.

In Eigner's poetry, as with Oppen's, the biographical aspect is crucial. Eigner was born with a severe case of cerebral palsy. His mobility was profoundly restricted (he was wheel-chair bound his entire life), and he had only the use of one finger and a thumb for the writing and spatial arrangement of his poetry (which has been published in a superb 4-volume edition by Stanford University [2010], with a Selected Poems forthcoming in 2016 from the University of Alabama Press's Modern and Contemporary Poetics Series, which I co-edit with Charles Bernstein). The introduction of a biographical perspective places the reading of Eigner's work within the realm of disability studies. It also asks us to consider what we mean by "the body" and its relationship to poetry, and to human consciousness. We might also think about – and attempt to embody ourselves – the heroism and persistence involved in Eigner's production of an astonishing body of poetry – over 75 books and broadsides! – and a very extensive correspondence. (In fact, in a graduate seminar I taught a few years ago, Jenifer Park, a fine poet and student, did embody Eigner's physical mode of composition, typing her research presentation as Eigner did, with limited use of one finger and a thumb, while using an old manual typewriter. It proved to be a superb learning experience, for her, and for us! Perhaps such work might be thought of as a very precise embodiment of ethical criticism?)

*

But often the considerations brought to bear on our reading and critical writing activities are, as Emerson would say about how we approach spiritual experience, at second-hand. Emerson's repeated call for spiritual experience at first-hand begins rather dramatically in his introduction to "Nature":

> Our age is retrospective. It builds the sepulchers of the fathers. It writes biographies, histories, and criticism. The foregoing generations beheld God and nature face to face; we, through their eyes. Why should not we also enjoy an original relation to the universe? Why should not we have a poetry and philosophy of insight and not of tradition, and a religion by revelation to us, and not the history of theirs? (21)

In "The Divinity School Address," he insists that our fundamental insights and intuitions "cannot be perceived at second hand" (104). Interestingly, in that same essay, Emerson suggests that "Europe has always owed to oriental genius its divine impulses" (104).

The shift in emphasis that I will be proposing in the remainder of my talk is from studying and analyzing the ethical decisions and actions of *others* to thinking of *oneself as already in the process of being an ethically engaged subject/agent.* (Perhaps the fictional or dramatic character of greatest interest is the reader/critic?)

*

Innovative poetry changes radically the nature of the reader's (and teacher's) authority in relation to the text. In the uncertainty, indeterminacy, and necessarily heuristic nature of such reading, there is a profound epistemological and ethical shift that takes place. (I would also argue that this kind of knowing not-knowing is, as presented in Lao Tzu's *Dao de jing*, an essentially Daoist mode of thinking.)

*

When I begin to think about ethical criticism, and how it might be practiced in the territory of innovative American poetry, I begin to take a few steps back so that I'm not immediately engaged in a series of ethical questions, observations, and decisions that already plunge me into the text itself and the ethical positions of the words, characters, and voices of the text. In other words, there are a variety of *ethical moments*, many of which occur and exist prior to the acts of reading and interpretation. Nonetheless, these too *are critical ethical moments*. And at this point I must note that my talk is addressed simultaneously to two different audiences, an American audience and a Chinese audience, each working under very different institutional and pedagogical circumstances.

For example, ethical decision-making with regard to poetry might be said to begin with a professor who is constructing a course and a syllabus. Many readers of poetry – particularly students who are not and will never be poets or specialists in the field of contemporary poetry – have a naïve assumption that poems somehow exist principally in anthologies and textbooks. (I believe it was David Antin who said "anthologies are to poems what zoos are to animals...") Even before we are thinking about the ethical positions taken within a particular poem, we need to consider the (small, or miniscule) economic domain of poetry. If the teacher has students encountering poems only in textbook-anthologies, then an ethical decision has been made that deprives readers of the knowledge and feel of what an actual *book* of contemporary poetry is. And if such books rarely make any money – for the publisher and the poet – the reader-student is also deprived of an important if baffling set of economic and ethical questions, such as, why would anyone devote a substantial portion of his/her life to poetry (writing and publishing) when the economics of it is not viable, or at least not given to profit? (As my poet-publisher-business-man-friend James Sherry puts it, "what's the quickest way to reduce the value of a blank sheet of paper? Begin to write a poem on it...") In the micro-economic ecosphere of contemporary poetry, a few classroom adoptions of a book published by a small or independent press can have a substantial impact. The same is not true of anthology adoptions or book adoptions for volumes published by huge mainstream corporate entities (such as Norton, or Macmillan, or Knopf…). Such classroom choices also have an impact on the poet's visibility (and ability to arrange paid readings, and campus visits).

Even within an anthology-textbook, the teacher faces a range of ethical decisions, nearly all of which might be deemed to fall under the heading of the ethics of diversity. Although in American political-ethical rhetoric, *diversity* usually means identity-centered difference – numbers of poets of color, poetry by women, poetry by LGBQT authors, perhaps some regional considerations, some class considerations – rarely do we foreground the equally important ethical consideration of the otherness of aesthetic difference.[v] (The anthology-textbooks themselves over the past forty years have shown increasing sensitivity to the former, more prevalent dimension of diversity, though only a small amount of consideration to aesthetic diversity.)

The teaching of new poetries also places the professor in a radically different position of authority, or non-authority, as the consideration of such poems is often profoundly collaborative, heuristic, and improvisationally exploratory.

*

Many years ago, in fact, when I was still an undergraduate student in the late 1960s, I ran into a statement that has stayed with me: *the student is educated by what the teacher is, not by his (or her) talk*. Such a statement, I believe it comes from Carl Jung, as it has resonated for me over many years, in my work as a teacher, a poet, and a critic, reminds me that it is not the postures we strike, not the didacticisms that we espouse, it is what we do in action – in the case of the classroom, in full view of the students – that is most pedagogical. For me, that ethical dimension of my conduct (as that fused identity of teacher, poet, and critic) takes on a particular urgency in relationship to what, especially in poetry, but also in music and the visual arts, is contemporary, i.e., of the present. Thus, what a teacher might manifest amounts to an ethics of attention and choice? There is an important ethics of engagement with the present that is crucial to the decisions and choices of a teacher-poet-reader-critic.

*

If we return for a moment to the *TLS* article about ethical criticism, we will find another important set of considerations, particularly as ethical criticism asks us to re-think the very nature of being human:

> Ethical literary critics argue that, in the history of human civilization, human beings have undergone a two-step selection procedure: natural selection and ethical selection. … But what truly distinguishes humans from other animals is the second selection: ethical selection, which helps to endow human beings with reason and ethical consciousness. This eventually turns them into ethical beings. (14-15)

I would like to make the argument that it is ethical to seek to understand better – through poetry – consciousness itself. Or, to put it more broadly, ethics amounts to a sincere and dedicated effort toward a deeper and better understanding of being.

*

An emphasis of ethical criticism that merits some consideration, particularly if ethical criticism is to have a life within the full range of poetic practice, is the place of reason. In the *TLS* article the authors discuss what is referred to as "the Sphinx factor":

> The Sphinx's combination of a human head and an animal body suggests, first of all, that the most important feature of a human image lies in its head, which stands for reason as a result of the evolutionary process, and reason is a decisive factor that enables human beings to be human beings. (15)

While *homo sapiens* is one common definition of human being, one might also (by way of Johan Huizinga's book, *Homo Ludens: A Study of the Play Element in Culture*, from 1950) choose to call us homo ludens, emphasizing the ludic or complex elements of playfulness that are equally characteristic of human beings. While in no way am I denying the value and importance of reason, there is also a compelling case to be made for an ethics which acknowledges and honors the limitations of reason, the humility and necessity of not-knowing, and the inherently incomplete nature of human knowing. (As I have been hinting, such a paradoxical affirmation lies at the heart of Daoist thinking, of Lao Tzu's *Dao de jing*, as opposed to the societal and behavioral pronouncements of Confucius.)

*

Drawing on Biwu Shang's "Ethical Criticism and Literary Studies: A Book Review Article about Nie's Work" (*CLCWeb: Comparative Literature and Culture* 15.7; 2013]), the perspective that I am eager to critique is the professed opposition or seeming incompatibility of ethical and aesthetic considerations:

> ...against the prevailing argument which sees literature as "an art of language" or as "an ideology of aesthetics," Nie considers literature as "an art of texts" and "a unique expression of ethics and morality within a certain historical period" (Ethical Literary Criticism and Other Issues 5). Further, according to Nie the primary function of literature is not aesthetics, but ethical enlightenment and education. These seemingly radical conceptions are now beginning to affect some traditional arguments about literature. Significantly, some college textbooks on literature and literary history in China have been compiled from an ethical perspective. (4)

But I don't think literature (and our relationship to it) presents us with a binary choice between ethics OR aesthetics. Of course, ethics matters. But "aesthetics" is not simply a matter of superficial (and changing) stylistic fads and adornments (like clothing accessories that go with each cultural era). At heart, aesthetics – how we go about our writing *now* – is epistemological and ontological. It involves (or ought to) the most serious of temporal (and ethical) matters: an attempt to engage reality as human consciousness *at a particular time* experiences it! (Again, this is why I much prefer

Lao Tzu's *Dao de jing* to Confucius' *Analects*, for the former is much
less prescriptive, less moralistic, more of an epistemological and
ontological investigation which acknowledges its own limitations to
speak with finality and clarity.)

As one of America's great (and I suspect little known in China) poet-
philosophers David Antin has stressed throughout his many years of
talk-poems: the present is difficult to locate, and it is most especially
difficult to locate the artistic present. In "how long is the present,"
Antin says,

> i have a taste
> for the present ...
> its a strong and peculiar
> taste   and the present is a difficult thing to have a taste for
> its very difficult because   in satisfying it the question
> i always have to ask myself is   what is the present and
> how long is it?   how long is the present?
> thats a question
> i take very seriously as a poet   i have a very strong commitment
> to the idea of the present   (158)

One might argue that at the heart of ontology, and of Zen practice,
and of the *Dao de jing*, is finding and developing a feeling for and a
partial understanding of the present, of the moment, of our specific
residence in this moment in time. Yet, most literary activity –
teaching, anthologies, textbooks, review-writing – is nostalgic and
directed toward a seemingly more understandable *past*, a reading
of and in texts where the conventions of expression and meaning-
making have a comfortable (even if complex) manner of signification.
One might call such an approach incomplete, or perhaps even
unethical.

Among American critics, the most important and best at elucidating
noteworthy contemporary writing is Marjorie Perloff (whose activity in
developing the CAAP conferences has been crucial!). In preparing
this talk, I returned to Marjorie's ground-breaking 1981 book, *The
Poetics of Indeterminacy: Rimbaud to Cage*. Marjorie understood
then, in noting that "Rimbaud was probably the first to write what
I shall call here the poetry of indeterminacy" (4), that to write

about innovative poetry would necessarily involve considering the very nature of signification itself (which, I would contend, is also fundamental to the *Dao de jing*). Thus Perloff comes to write about works that are "endlessly frustrating our longing for certainty" and writing and art projects that "derive their force from their refusal to 'mean' in conventional ways" (34). (As you will see when I turn to the *Dao de jing*, it is perhaps a profoundly Chinese epistemology or ontology to engage what is enigmatic and indeterminate and deeply paradoxical in its nature – a cosmos and an experience of being that evades final pronouncements, and is thus best suited to the flexible modes of saying that are essential to poetry?) Perloff, who was one of the first to recognize the importance of Antin's work, notes that Antin declares " ' the one thing I believe a poet ought to do is respect what he doesn't understand, respect its unintelligibility' " (302). The profoundly heuristic nature of the truly new, the truly present-engaged poetry, will always seem and feel to us, initially, to be baffling. And it will also compel us to re-investigate what we mean by "meaning" itself.

Perhaps the best writing ever on the difficulties of locating the artistic/aesthetic present occurs in Gertrude Stein's lecture "Composition as Explanation" (1926). Though Stein's concern is principally with beauty, the reception and rejection of new works in new modes of artistic composition (due to the allegedly irritating nature of the new), and the subsequent strangely rapid transition in the perception and appreciation of the work from outlaw to classic, her remarks, like Antin's and Perloff's, also point to an ethics of locating or searching for the artistic present. First and foremost, such activity – trying to find the artistic present – matters for reasons that are ontological:

> The only thing that is different from one time to another is what is seen and what is seen depends upon how everybody is doing everything. This makes the thing we are looking at very different and this makes what those who describe it make of it, it makes a composition[.] (Selected Writings, 513)

Both the work of art and *how we **conduct** our lives* are called by Stein *compositions*: "Each period of living differs from any other period of living not in the way life is but in the way life is conducted and that authentically speaking is composition" (517). Thus, to know the present modes of composition would give us insight into what we see, the nature of our present life in time, and how we are conducting (or composing) our lives. Why does this *not* happen? Laziness: "and as every one is naturally indolent why naturally they don't see" (515). As I have been suggesting, this lack of awareness of present modes of new composition is a serious pedagogical matter, and thus an ethical matter. It might also be argued that how we respond to the otherness – the strangeness – of innovative art mirrors or rhymes with our treatment of human beings (and cultures) whose otherness and difference challenge our compassion and acceptance. Our response to textual difference – to the new composition – is no doubt every bit an occasion steeped in ethics as it is a merely cognitive or interpretive moment.

Another way to think about the composing of our lives takes us into the murky terrain of that elusive term *consciousness*. I would suggest – at the risk of being unfashionably sincere and naked – that ultimately poetry is "about" consciousness – really, a manifestation of consciousness. Which is also why poetry must and does continue to change (and why, as Stein, Antin, Perloff, and Bernstein advocate, we ought to pay plenty of attention to newly emerging modes of composition). Because the nature of human consciousness – perhaps at no time in human history as today – is changing. And poetry is, at heart, part of our effort to understand, explore, and manifest that (changing) consciousness. Poetry allows us to develop a *feel* for consciousness, which is inextricable from a deepened awareness of being and time, and deepened awareness and knowledge of the ongoing composition which we call perception.

While I have been advocating attention to such manifestations in the present – to innovative poetry of this moment – the roots, particularly in Chinese literature, for such a function for poetry and for writing generally go very deep. While Lao Tzu's *Dao de jing* includes plenty of advice about how to govern effectively, the enduring strength of this work (which other than the Bible may be the most translated work on earth?) is in its simply stated and infinitely complex engagement with the nature of being. As David Hinton suggests in his introduction to Lao Tzu's work,

> Although its inexplicable nature is a central motif in the *Tao Te Ching*, we might approach Lao Tzu's Way by speaking of it at its deep ontological level, where the distinction between Presence (Being) and Absence (Nonbeing) arises. … The ontological structure of Way is replicated in the structure of human consciousness, thoughts arising from the same generative emptiness as the ten thousand things. … It is here in the depths of consciousness that Way can be experienced directly through the practice of meditation. You can watch the process of Way as thought burgeons forth from the emptiness and disappears back into it, or you can simply dwell in that undifferentiated emptiness, that generative realm of Absence. (18-19)

Lao Tzu's consideration of the Way (*Dao*) contrasts sharply with the more practical, behavioral engagement with Way found in his contemporary Confucius' *Analects*. Raymond Dawson, in his introduction to the *Analects*, suggests that Confucius uses the Way "to refer either to the ideal course of conduct for an individual or to an ideal political organization" (xxiv-xxv). In the *Dao de jing*, we study the Way for its own sake, and to engage a generative emptiness that may help us to understand better our own nature.

Throughout Lao Tzu's *Dao de jing*, we find advocacy of an ongoing engagement with the nature of consciousness, a deepening awareness of being, which is a mirroring of *wu wei* (and which does carry with it ethical and behavioral and even governmental implications, though that is not his primary focus): "If you're nothing doing what you do/ all things will be governed well" (3.12-13; p. 35) From Lao Tzu's perspective, nothing else can "compare to sitting still in Way's company" (62.10; p. 100). He could also be describing the often vexing experience of encountering a new mode of contemporary art, an innovative poetry that defies our expectations and habits. He asks, "Who's murky enough to settle slowly into pure clarity,/ and who still enough to awaken slowly into life?" (15.13-14; p. 47).

What we encounter in the *Dao de jing* is analogous to the reading experience of innovative poetry – an enigmatic encounter that requires patience, open-mindedness (in Zen terminology, beginner's mind), and the development of an ability (negative capability?) to live in uncertainty and with an ethical humility that suggests the incompleteness of our understandings. Thus the *Dao de jing* begins, "A Way called *Way* isn't the perennial Way./ A name that names isn't the perennial name" (1.1-2; p. 33). And yet, "Way remains hidden and nameless,/ but it alone nourishes and brings to completion" (41.21-22; p. 79). Lao Tzu's great poem is a cautionary tale regarding the perils of success, power, and will, and thus it carries with it serious ecological and political implications, which, of course, are thus also pedagogical and ethical implications. It is poetry – much like the best of contemporary innovative poetry – that both asks us to give it our fullest effort, intellect, and attention, all the while realizing, "The further you explore, the less you know.// So it is that a sage knows by going nowhere,/ names by seeing nothing,/ perfects by doing nothing" (47.5-8; p. 85).

Thus I am proposing an additional dimension to what we think of as ethical criticism, and it involves a reading process that, by necessity, is inconclusive, not confined to what is reasonable, and knows quite certainly that certainty will not be the outcome. If it yields conclusions, they will not be Confucian nuggets of wisdom; they will be conclusions that undo themselves. It is an ethical not-knowing, which, nonetheless, is what ethical learning amounts to: an ongoing conversation, ever leading to more questions and more comments.

To conclude, let me illustrate what such ethical criticism might look like by reading a poem by Larry Eigner.

May 29 71   # 5 0 7

paper
  a cut map
    beautiful
    land
      beds
        tree
       the air
         to dance in
       time
      what ground
        stretches out
        dancing, you feel like
         dancing

        so many winds blowing

forest   the mind
      flight
      the sun
         on the open
        then the earth
         wall

(The Collected Poems of Larry
Eigner, Volume III 1966-1978, p.1012)

Larry Eigner's poetry presents us with a perpetual changing of direction, often a swerving from word to word, from line to line. The page becomes a highly malleable (seemingly infinitely so) locale for an instance of grace of mind, a turning about that is highly particular, idiosyncratic (and a perhaps simultaneously universal?) movement of consciousness in a complex relationship with language.

At nearly every moment of Eigner's #507 we have the possibility, and often the actuality, of a change in direction. Perhaps our own engaged questioning allows us to move with the movement of his poem. "paper" – is it this paper, that is, the one where the poem is being written? Or perhaps the paper that is, as the next line suggests, "a cut map," and is a poem, this poem, then a kind of "cut map"? cut out or from what? And the poem calls it "beautiful" – is the beauty what we are seeing emerge as the poem delineates itself, or is it something else that is more generally beautiful? What follows is a discrete series of things, a brief descending catalog – "land/ beds/ tree/ the air" – are they, each, what is beautiful, or perhaps they are beautiful, as the next line suggests, "to dance in". But how does one dance in (or with) a series of descending general nouns? Perhaps the poem is the moment of our dancing, a poem that swerves, that delights in its own possibilities of movement, "to dance in/ time", the dance, then, being a moving in space and time. The dance takes place at least two times: in the time of the poem's composition, and in the time of our reading of it (as we dance with and in its movement, its turning).

Our being, then, takes place here, in space and time, in a place of "land" and "beds" and "tree" and "the air," and we dance and we are upon "what ground" – the place that "stretches out," and which calls to us to consider "dancing, you feel like/dancing". That ground – as in Heidegger's thinking – is defined by our relationship to being and time. The ground, then, is a mixture of something we think through and about, at once familiar, present, and profoundly strange and enigmatic. A known place, but equally an ignored and unknowable thing, inextricably part of our own enigmatic nature. A ground that we may glimpse or sense in some poems.

These lines then are perhaps a kind of consecutive descent – a cascade, a waterfall – of an ongoing line of thinking, an initial direction of movement that does not swerve or sway too far from its initial impulse and its initial direction. But then there is that last line of this section: "so many winds blowing". What winds? That general "western wind" of an ongoing poetic tradition? A wind that might be upon and across "land" and "beds" and in a "tree" and essential and resident of "the air"? Or perhaps the "so many winds blowing" is true for any instant of consciousness, especially one manifesting itself on "paper/ a cut map"?

After a considerable open space – the largest of the poem, this "cut map" cut from an instance of awareness in space and time – we encounter the most remarkable turn of the poem: "forest   the mind". It is an apposition, which, in retrospect – the shift in direction allows us to look back – has been mildly implicit earlier in the poem, so that we now might consider another understanding of "what ground": a support or space or entity that allows us to hold in awareness "land" "beds" "tree" and "the air", and to dance with these seen and named locales. That forest/mind, wherein we find "so many winds blowing" – and this goes to the heart of much of Eigner's poetry which can be read as an ongoing phenomenology, a mapping or engaging of the rapidity of perception and the complexity and grace of seeing's dance with language and naming. It is an exhilarating sense of mind, which moves us upward perceptually, to "flight" and "the sun", a dancing "on the open", which, ultimately, comes back down to "then the earth/ wall".

Perhaps it is the lack of connectives from word to word and even more so from line to line, perhaps it is the lack of a typical authorial pronoun that makes the poem on the page feel like a mobile, like a suspension of words and phrases of varying weight, in charged and multiple relationships to one another. Thus from almost every line to the next, we are either shifting or re-directing our attention or taking a leap, learning as we read the poem – and tutored precisely by the painstaking arrangement of the words on the page – how to travel a similar perceptual path.

*

Quite amazing, inspiring, and pertinent, then, to consider that Eigner, in spite of his severe case (from birth) of cerebral palsy, composed over 3,000 poems, "producing his typescripts on his 1940 Royal manual typewriter using only his right index finger and thumb to create shifting constellations of words in space whose musical and visual designs are realized in a language at once immediate and highly abstract" (editors' jacket note, Vol. III).

As we take this second major turn in our reading – an exploration and recognition of the poet's physical state, and a shift toward an embodied sense of the poem's composition – perhaps our reading of the poem changes somewhat. In light of Eigner's cerebral palsy and the difficult process of typing his poems, do we read lines like "dancing, you feel like/ dancing" differently? Do we read differently knowing he could not dance, or does the poem itself become that dancing (which, perhaps, is how we would read the poem all along without the re-consideration brought about by our knowledge of the poet's physical circumstance)? Do we return early in the poem to the cascade of general nouns and see now that "beds" is quite different than "land", "tree", and "the air", and may indicate, obliquely, the poet's physical location?

*

As Emmanuel Levinas has suggested, "we exist in a circuit of intelligence with the real" (*Entre Nous*, p. 4). Innovative and somewhat baffling contemporary poetry offers us a place, in language, to experience and respond to – *without mastery* – the complexity of the real. Or, as Lao Tzu writes,

> Honoring Way and treasuring Integrity
> isn't obedience to command,
> it's occurrence perennially appearing of itself.

(51. ll. 7-9, p. 89)

In reading this one poem by Larry Eigner, I am sketching an ethical reading practice based on humility and limitation, as we come up against our not-knowing (try as we might to know). Such reading places us within an ethics of paradox and doubleness – of profound curiosity and delving, along with the recognition of the partial and indeterminate nature of the activity. That ongoing conversation where we collaborate in articulating our observations and questions, our tentative expressions of signification and meaning, *is knowing*, and its generative questions and limitations are a respectful and ethical way of being in the world.

Notes

[i] This essay is an expanded version of the keynote address that I presented in Jinan on November 29, 2015, for the 4th Convention of the Chinese/American Association for Poetry and Poetics.

[ii] *Selected Poems and Essays of Hank Lazer,* Central China Normal University Press: 2015. For Professor Nie's Preface, see pp, 1-7.

[iii] "Zui Wei Qun Ti." *Poetry Monthly* (October 2013): 39-47. Hefei:Poetry Monthly Press, 2013.

[iv] Oppen is quoting from a letter sent to him by Rachel Blau DuPlessis.

[v] At the 4th CAAP conference, I note with great pleasure the contributions of participants Dr. Maryemma Graham and Dr. Lauri Ramey, each of whom in their presentations, pedagogy, and publishing have done noteworthy work to promote both elements of diversity. The two anthologies – *Every Goodbye Ain't Gone: An Anthology of Innovative Poetry by African Americans* (2006) and *What I Say: Innovative Poetry by Black Writers in America* (2015), edited by Lauri Ramey and Aldon Nielsen – provide tremendous resources for and evidence of the great variety and excellence of innovative poetry by African American poets.

Works Cited

Antin, David. *How Long is the Present: Selected Talk Poems of David Antin.* Ed. Stephen Fredman. Albuquerque: U of New Mexico Pr, 2014.

Baker, William and Shang Biwu. "Fruitful Collaborations: Ethical Literary Criticism in Chinese Academe." *Times Literary Supplement,* 31 July 2015: 14-15.

Bernstein, Charles. "Pitch of Poetry." *Forum for World Literature Studies,* Vol. 7, No. 3 (September 2015): 426-438.

Eigner, Larry. *The Collected Poems of Larry Eigner,* Volumes 1-4. Eds. Robert Grenier and Curtis Faville. Stanford: Stanford U Pr, 2010.

Emerson, Ralph Waldo. *Selections from Ralph Waldo Emerson.* Ed. Stephen E. Whicher. Boston: Houghton Mifflin Company, 1960.

Huizinga, Johan. *Homo Ludens: A Study of the Play Element in Culture.* Boston: Beacon Pr, 1955.

Lazer, Hank. "The Peculiarities of the Making of Cross-Cultural Literary History: Poetry of George Oppen and Larry Eigner." *Foreign Literature Studies* (Wuhan, China), Vol. 35, No. 5 (October 2013): 9-22.

Levinas, Emmanuel. *Entre Nous.* Translated by Michael B. Smith and Barbara Harshaw. New York: Columbia U Pr, 1998.

Oppen, George. *New Collected Poems.* Ed. Michael Davidson. New York: New Directions, 2002.

Perloff, Marjorie. *The Poetics of Indeterminacy: Rimbaud to Cage.* Princeton: Princeton U Pr, 1981.

Shang, Biwu. "Ethical Criticism and Literary Studies: A Book Review Article about Nie's Work." *CLCWeb: Comparative Literature and Culture* 15.7 [2013]: http://docs.lib.purdue.edu/cgi/viewcontent.cgi?article=2372&context=clcweb

Stein, Gertrude. *Selected Writings of Gertrude Stein.* "Composition as Explanation." Pages 511-523. New York: Vintage, 1990.

A Thread

Joe Ashby Porter

Aaron the Moor in Shakespeare's first tragedy *Titus Andronicus* boasts of a wonderful congeries of heinous deeds culminating in

> Oft have I digged up dead men from their graves
> And set them upright at their dear friends' door
> Even when their sorrows almost was forgot,
> And on their skins, as on the bark of trees,
> Have with my knife carvèd with Roman letters
> 'Let not your sorrow die, though I am dead.'

"Oft'? Even among the enormities of late classical Rome, many paraded in this play's own Grand Guignol, municipal authorities seem strangely remiss not to have noticed a plague of so singular a *modus operandi*. And is Aaron's "men" meant to imply that dear friendship can only be male, or merely that the male torso provides the preferred writing surface? Much else here repays scrutiny, and in particular Aaron's specification of "Roman letters." Roman in contrast to what? Greek perhaps, the quasi-second language of the empire, or Gothic, presumably used in Tamora's native realm, or the

Arabic of Aaron's, which the chime with Aaron's own name might favor, along with its status as his native script.

Aaron's ethnicity, by the way, itself sounds in the middle syllable of his paramour Tamora, whose name may have figured in Julie Taymor's choice of the play for her neo-Fellini *Titus*, which unaccountably cuts out Aaron almost altogether. As for the Moor-Rome phonetic inversion, when spoken it sets Aaron against his adoptive city, while as text it shimmers with the arbitrariness of direction in horizontal script, left-to-right in Latin and English and the reverse in Arabic.

More in any case is involved here, as always when Shakespeare writes of writing and reading. Long ago James Calderwood showed how much the opposition between page and stage, between the written and spoken word, vexes the young Shakespeare, who takes writing for the public stage as a prostitution and mutilation of his verbal power, a situation he embodies in the nightmare back-formation of Lavinia's writing with her tongueless mouth. Hence the logical tailspin when Aaron tells of using Roman letters for his inscription: while his nominally Latin words are in fact English, the script itself is truly both Latin and English at once.

Aaron's aporia toys with the necessary and hence normally invisible convention of translation, by which the spoken language of a story set outside any given audience's language community must stand in for the implied language of the speakers. Here as generally Shakespeare's way is to foreground some of what goes without saying. He does so early with Aaron and intermittently later, as with *Henry V* where he uses the convention in most of the French scenes written in English, yet also almost playfully provides a French scene written entirely in French. *TA* produces a different effect, and there nothing like toying, when Lavinia with her mouth writes "Stuprum"—as though the gravity of the crime committed against her has ruptured the convention of translation, as happens again in the next Roman play with "Et tu, Brute."

Although Shakespeare read several foreign languages, the only one he used for more than a phrase is French, the language he might first have imagined seeing his work translated into, if ever he dreamed of such matters. It was not to be. We have record of only one translation published before his death, an anonymous German *Merchant of Venice* from 1611 that he could scarcely have seen, and his work does not appear in French until the mid-eighteenth century, nor down the centuries have the French proved particularly receptive to him. Nevertheless he repeatedly consulted and probably owned the delightful French-English language manual, John Eliot's *Ortho-epia Gallica* (1593), which he consulted not only for the French of *H5* but also in his composition of *King Lear*, possibly envisioning a scene for Cordelia in France.

Eliot also provided the odd nugget that stuck like a burr in Shakespeare's mind. Thereby hangs a tale about the most famous crux in English literature, in Hostess Quickly's account of Falstaff's death when she says that "his nose was as sharp as a pen, and a Table of green fields." In the eighteenth century Lewis Theobald emended the apparent nonsense to "and 'a babbled of green fields." That speculative emendation stood for two and a half centuries, with no foundation other than its apparent sense and the certainty that in Shakespeare's hand "'a babbled" could easily be misread by a compositor as "a Table." Finally in 1986 a young Shakespearean announced that he had found an explanation for Theobald's emendation, in Eliot's near collocation of "babilards" (Fr. babblers) and "green fields"—the young Shakespearean in question being my alter ego Joseph A. Porter. He, emboldened by this early breakthrough, has continued to explore and expound upon Shakespeare and, with fellow editors of the New Variorum *Othello*, hopes to complete the project soon.

Joseph A. has occupied himself over the decades with Shakespeare's Mercury, the god of writing, and with distinctive Shakespearean spectral scriptiveness, and with arguments by Lukas Erne and others that Shakespeare wrote his plays to be enjoyed not only from the stage but also from the page, as text. Of late Joseph A. has mused willy-nilly over those moments in *The Tempest* when "Shakespeare" glimmers just beneath the surface, as with Prospero's "the strong-based promontory/Have I made *shake* and by the *spurs* plucked up/The pine and cedar."

Meanwhile I myself Joe Ashby have pursued my career in fiction writing, I too buoyed and nourished by Shakespeare, and sometimes in ways I understand only long after the fact, if then. When my first novel *Eelgrass*, riffing on *The Tempest*, was accepted by James Laughlin for his legendary press New Directions shortly before his retirement, he asked me to curtail one chapter (no problem) and to replace the title, which he found "odd." Titles are never easy for me and this one had cost some agonizing, but of course I bit the bullet and spent the ensuing summer obsessing over contenders, almost nightly falling asleep sure that I had finally made the right choice only to realize the next morning that no, back to the drawing board. Because like *The Tempest* the novel transpires on an island and concerns kinds of territorial boundaries, I had titled it after a plant native to intertidal zones. In the end I threw up my hands and sent Laughlin the much blander *Fortunate Islanders*—only to learn by return mail that he had grown accustomed to *Eelgrass* and preferred it.

The novel with its Prospero-less island dials forward Shakespeare's deep protofeminism, and it also channels his arm's-length francophilia, not only in a silly erotic subplot set in a French country house but also in its title. As I saw with a start years after publication, *Eelgrass* puns on *île grasse—grasse* as in mardi *gras—* which might serve uncannily well for a title should the novel ever have the good fortune to appear in French.

To date only my novel *The Near Future* has been translated out of English, and it into only one language, French. Joëlle Losfeld chose it for her imprint at Gallimard, France's (the world's?) premier publisher of literary fiction, and she commissioned its translation *Le future proche* by Bernard Hoepffner, one of France's most distinguished literary translators, for publication in Gallimard's centennial year, during which the house's street became rue Gallimard. Recently I have been absorbed with kinds of spectral translatedness in several fiction writers, including Lydia Davis, herself a literary translator from French to English, whose distinctive English can read like translation, and Ha Jin, who writes fiction in his second language, English, and has begun to translate some of it into his first, Chinese, much as Beckett once did with French. As for me, in collaboration with Joseph A. Porter I have nearly completed an eminently translatable memoir, *Deep France*, about our multifarious engagements with Shakespeare and with France.

And speaking of engagements, happily mine of forty-five years with Frenchman Yves Orvoën has ended in marriage. On 12/13/14 when we tied the knot in Paris, in a hall decorated with mythological and allegorical murals, there behind and above the deputy mayor stood none other than Shakespeare's, France's, and my own tutelary deity, Mercury himself, larger than life, nearly nude, and attentive if noncommittal.

Solving For X

Paul Pines

PART I – SPINNING THE CLOTH

1 – *Root meanings*

I have been asked to write something about biography. Dictionary definitions agree that a biography refers to an account of a life written by someone other than the subject. I want to pursue an enlarged notion of biography, where the focus can be on an individual, group, era, a discipline, movement, idea, or any entity that unfolds discretely. I realize as I write this sentence that I am performing a biographical act. I am proposing to write a biography of biography. If we include subgenres of Autobiography, Confession, Memoir, and contemporary conflations like Cultural Journalism, whether the exercise emphasizes objectivity or personal observation, the patterns revealed are empirically recognizable in ways that either directly or mysteriously affect our lives.

Lewis Thomas' *Lives of a Cell*, is a prime example. Published in 1974, this biography of a cell explores the building block of our organic world by describing both its perceived behaviors and the interior process that generates them. A key observation is that the patterns shaped by life forms within that cell are not derived from it. These "organelles," like mitochondria and chloroplasts, exist within the cell symbiotically to their mutual benefit. Thomas extends this view of interdependent processes throughout nature, including our fascination with computers, space travel, and technology, and cites language itself as an organism. What starts as the biography of a cell, leads to a larger vision in which we too can be understood as discrete organisms within a larger host-like organization of information sharing: the Earth itself as a living cell.

Thomas describes the processes within the cell as a way of storing energy and information. This may also apply to larger organizations of information as the basis for patterns of behavior in human beings. The psyche of an individual is shaped by early attachments, traumas, introjected relationships, discrete "complexes," that function like organelles in a cell to make each of us unique, and partially unknown to ourselves.

Thomas might say that both the known and unknown parts of ourselves are stored in the psyche as information and energy. Biographical narratives probe both the subject's observable behaviors, and the latent patterns that shape them. They compel our attention most when they correspond to our own experience. We know that patterns exist within the host as they do in nature at large and hope to recognize them, like Fibonacci's numerical sequence in leaf formation, the Golden Ratio in a chambered nautilus, or Pythagorean frequency intervals of planetary vibrations recorded by NASA. Biography may resolve itself in such a snapshot, or give us a glimpse of what connects us to the mystery we pose and occupy. Language, which Thomas suggests is a symbiotic system we contain that allows us to store information in complex ways, unlike ants and bees. Through language-driven narrative we are able to reveal latent information, and a concomitant release of energy. This is often experienced and an epiphany, or illumination. We are drawn to it, equations solving for ourselves. It is a fundamental drive of the organism. Or why go there?

*

Given the release of energy when what is latent emerges, an enlarged notion of Biography may be found in its etymology:

Bios: Gk, n. Life.
Graphos: v. to write.

Based on these root-words, Biography is the act of writing about a life. Taking my cue from Thomas, I suggest that Biography can be construed as life writing about itself. It is an expression of the fundamental drive to bring to light what is hidden and in doing so to release the energy that delivers information from latency to awareness. I suggest that information and energy are complimentary, just as on a quantum level sub-atomic particles are interchangeable with waves. Plato spoke of this as Eros, fundamental creative energy that strives to make itself clear. The release of energy/information in biographical exploration is an experience of Eros that balances our fear of death by reminding us of our continuity as a species. By the same measure, Biography recognizes the allure of death, Thanatos—celebrates it as an aspect of itself. Opposites are in constant play in this narrative. Biography holds the mirror up to life; through it we participate in an activity that employs language in search of the truth beyond language. As the poet George Oppen put it in his poem, *Leviathan*, "The truth is also the search for it."

2 – Language & meaning

When asked if a man can adopt a standpoint outside the psyche, the Swiss psychiatrist C.G. Jung responded: "He may assert that he can, but the assertion does not create a point outside, and were he there he would have no psyche." (*Letters Vol. 1*, pp 555-557). Many in the post-modern camp tell us that there is no way to talk about meaning apart from language. The danger in this assertion is the conclusion that language is meaning, that there is nothing meaningful apart from what can be said. But standing outside of psyche is not the same as standing outside of language. Mind makes meaning in a much more complex way. We are constantly at the threshold of meaning, latent and expressed. Biography responds to this more directly than any other literary form. In the broadest cultural terms, biographical exploration is embedded in the transformational mission of Myth, which the Greeks understood as a truth so profound one stutters when attempting to articulate directly.

3- *The Monomyth—a self-organizing system*

Joseph Campbell in his classic *Hero with a Thousand Faces* (1949), opines that what he calls the monomyth of the Hero's Journey represents the basic structure of all narrative. The argument is that this structure replicates the arc of our lives, and calls to each of us to become the hero of his/her individual journey. By extension, it follows that Biography, as life writing about itself, follows these contours.

We can summarize this structure as one in which the hero starts with a problem that makes the current state in which he/she exists untenable, and receives a call to address this by striking out on a journey into the unknown. Flanked by allies and formidable adversaries, the hero is challenged to the point of near defeat, only to be saved by the intervention of an ally or inspiration that allows him/her to overcome the obstacle and return home transformed to establish a new equilibrium. This pattern is echoed by Eric Erikson's eight stages of human development, Chaos theory, the process by which self-organizing systems in nature are transformed to reach a new equilibrium, and Elizabeth Kubler Ross' five stages of grief.

James Hillman observes that in the Hero's Journey the main character is not the hero, but the archetypal structure of the myth itself. Hercules' labors, Odysseus at Erebus, Psyche's descent into Hades, and Parsifal's trail to the Grail Castle are all there in the service of a greater meaning. My own memoir, *My Brother's Madness* (2007), describes a deepening descent into the dark issues siblings project onto each other. Like Odysseus at Erebus, I attempted to engage with family ghosts to shed light on the forces that flowered in my brother's psychotic delusion. Even in such an intimate formulation, my journey through that Brooklyn childhood finds a place in Campbell's equation, Biography as a transformative myth.

4 – *Summoning the shades*

Homer's Iliad, the epic Biography of Greek civilization, predates the written word (800 BC). His second biographical account, the *Odyssey*, focuses on an individual through stages of a journey that begins when one civilization, Troy, has fallen, and the unity of the one that brought it down, the Achaeans, is questionable. In the Tenth Book of the *Odyssey*, Ulysses is prompted by the sorceress, Circe, to visit Erebus, a twilight zone between Earth and Hades. He follows her instruction and sails the deep waters of Oceanus to a land "enshrouded in mist and darkness which the sun's rays never pierce." There, sitting on one side of a trench he fills with the blood of the black ewe and ram that Circe has left him for this purpose, Odysseus waits as shades rise in great number drawn by their appetite for blood. By holding them off with his sword, he allows each to drink one at a time, questions them closely, including slain comrades, and his mother, whom he tries unsuccessfully to embrace. The dead have questions for him, as well: Achilles comes forward to ask after his father, and his son. A few have requests. Elpenor, who fell from Circe's roof in a drunken stupor and broke his neck, reminds Odysseus that his corpse remains unburied. The blind Theban prophet, Tiresias, whom Odysseus had come to see, greets Odysseus on arrival, and instructs him how to conduct himself. Tiresias tells him that on this threshold, the dead require blood to speak. If the visitor does not let them drink, the dead will disappear. When questioned how to get back to his home in Ithaca safely, Tiresias reveals that Odysseus has angered Poseidon by blinding his son, the Cyclops, and that he alone will survive the journey.

Holding the golden scepter that marks his status in the Underworld, Tiresias might well have confirmed the notion that Biography involves using language to call forth what is beyond language at the cusp of the underworld.

Homer might've agreed that Biography functions as an offering that allow the ancestors to speak—to invite the meaning latent in the particulars of our lives to reveal itself. At the trench separating Erebus from the world above, Odysseus learns that a dialogue with the dead works both ways. Those who approach the portal with a degree of openness, answering as well as asking questions, discover what the shades long to know, their unfinished business. We read biographies listening for their voices. Biography, in its own right, is a shade waiting to speak to us if we understand the point of the visit.

5- *Fragments*

We make a mistake to view Biography as a strictly narrative literary structure, with a beginning, middle and end. As a record of human experience, we can locate the biographical intention in the genealogies found in Hesiod's *Theogony*, or Genesis 10, recording the sons of Noah in the Hebrew Bible. Or a fragment of the letter written by the Egyptian Pharaoh, Amenhotep III, to the Babylonian king, Kadasman-Enlil (ca. 1374 BC), in the Amarna series: *Now I have heard the message you sent to me concerning it, saying "You seek my daughter for your wife and my sister who my father gave to you is there with you but no one has seen her now, whether she is alive whether she is dead."* There are the makings of a memoir here. Consider this ancient Greek epitaph that Rhodope inscribed on her stone dog house for her beloved pet, not far from her own grave: *This is the tomb of the dog, Stephanos, who perished, Whom Rhodope shed tears for and buried like a human. I am the dog Stephanos, and Rhodope set up a tomb for me.* Canine biography. Or graffiti from the basilica in Pompeii: *Virgula to her friend Tertius: you are disgusting!*

Even the most mundane and indecipherable artifacts reveal a mystery that impinges on bio/graphos, draws us to the threshold of conscious expression. How the information comes to us determines the way we respond. Under the enlarged umbrella of Biography there is Autobiography, and related forms such as Confession and Memoir. But for pure power, the Fragment that challenges us to fill in what is not already visible often reads more powerfully than the narrative whole. The invisible hand of time and clash of civilizations has shattered what had been well composed. We are left with pieces that have come down to us as voices on the threshold of Erebus, wanting to engage us, waiting to feed.

Heraclitus, in the 6th Century BC, anticipated Einstein's conclusion that energy is the essence of matter, and C. G. Jung's unity of opposites. His major work, *On Nature*, has been lost to us. What we have put together are the pieces saved by others. Hippolytus saved us this fragment: *Men do not know how what is at variance agrees with itself. It is an attunement of opposite tension, like that of the bow and the lyre.*

What we know about Heraclitus is that he liked to meditate

by a stream, in front of a bonfire. Absent his complete work, which might have been a compelling philosophical argument, we have fragments that resonate through space/time. Each Fragment is a mini-Biography. The voice embedded in the words comes to us with an astounding immediacy, suspended between what's said and left unsaid. I hear it in this shard of Heraclitus preserved by Diogenes Laertius: *Wisdom is one thing. It is to know the thought by which all things are steered through all things.*

PART II – WEAVING THE CLOTH

6 – *Confession and Memoir*

> *Blessed is the man against whom the LORD counts no iniquity, and in whose spirit there is no deceit. For when I kept silent, my bones wasted away through my groaning all day long. For day and night your hand was heavy upon me; my strength was dried up as by the heat of summer. Selah.*
>
> Psalm 32:1-5

Confession may be one of the most powerful drives of the species. It presents as an acknowledgment of wrong doing, or a telling disclosure. We commonly view it as an integrative function, through which the confessor seeks absolution or atonement. Withholding a confession can result in a perilous loss of balance and dangerous behavior. Confession may be the bottom line truth about ourselves as we understand it. Some find it a refuge when all other options have failed. Long before the Church Fathers institutionalized the confessional as the glue that held the framework of Mother Church together, the ancient Egyptian Mysteries of Osiris weighed individual souls against a feather. The Greek Mysteries at Eleusis recognized confession as the primary protocol for all their initiates.

What do we make of a creature that confesses itself to itself in order to understand what has already happened and to anticipate what might become of it?

Confession is best suited to Autobiography, a tale in the first person. Unlike Biography, the story of a life written by another, the narrative needn't unfold in a linear fashion that invokes the objective point of view to arrive at its destination. There is no need to verify through a number of primary sources and extensive research. Autobiography, and its subset, Confession, and Memoir, are subjective forms of self-disclosure, often best told by the untethering time and space, regarding them as moveable pieces used to reveal underlying patterns. Rather than hold onto a tight chronological rein, loosening them may let the story unfold in psychological space, where the past, present and future form a mosaic that reveals otherwise invisible connections between events. Linear cause and effect sequence rides to its destination on a monorail that may work well for the conventional Biography. In Autobiography, the focus on motive enlists underlying psychological forces that may haunt the reader long after the last page has been turned.

Confession, in particular, emphasizes the revelation of the shadow, the unconscious vectors that set our lives in motion. In the course of exploring them, the confessor my emerge as both the victim and perpetrator of the forgotten crimes, the insults sustained during childhood, the punishing responses to self and others that once disclosed allow for atonement. Confession invites us to understand that as terrible as the situation may have been, or as trivial, there is a purpose. Though even as purpose is restored, there may remain a lingering doubt, a shadow in the room.

In the realm of popular detective fiction, there is a reason why the most prosaic thriller is anchored in confession. From Poe to Patterson, confession makes the motives clear, restores the mask of civility on what had been the most heinous crime. But behind the safety of the convention, the reader is left with the suspicion that the unspeakable potentials of human behavior await to shatter the illusion of order.

In our first great *Confession* by St. Augustine in 397 AD, the tradition of self-disclosure is launched by the author's theft of a pear from his neighbor's garden. The mystery to be solved is not about the theft. The act speaks for itself. But what compelled a sixteen year old who had enough to eat to steal food, and then throw away the pear half eaten. What is being confessed is valuable in that it deepens our understanding of who is confessing.

7 - Who tells the story?

Confession and Memoir are always solving for X: who is telling this story? There is a significant difference in focus between these two. Memoir uses a broad canvas in which the actor's world is a character. One might say that the hero of the memoir is Memory, and essential in revealing what is being sought. Confession is a vehicle for the teller who, unburdening his dark heart, is solving for the missing pieces of the puzzle in himself. The form rides on the promise of the teller to reveal it in the telling. The confession starts at the entrance to the underworld, where a dark event emerges like a ghost, feeds on blood, and then slaps the confessor awake. In a realized work, the reader also feels the blow. The impact can change the way we think about things for centuries.

Consider Augustine, that boy who stole a pear from his neighbor's garden for motives he could not at the time understand, but revealed in the course of his confession. Through self-examination around the issue of innocence and guilt, the thieving thinker arrived at a far more universal conclusion about the moral condition of the species. What started as the theft of a pear from a neighbor's garden, drove Augustine to question the existence of original innocence in the entire species. The original crime so resonant of his own had been perpetrated by a serpentine curiosity that prompted him to eat of the forbidden apple in Eden. That act, sealed in our DNA, revealed the underlying motive of Augustine theft. We are all, he concluded, born with the legacy of *Original Sin*.

Confession requires not only a speaker, but a dedicated listener, one who can understand and absolve the penitent. To whom is Augustine confessing? There are a number of levels to this. First, he is confessing to himself. Then, to the reader, who assumes a privileged position as witness. Finally, Augustine's *Confession*, as he indicates throughout, is informed by the voice he identifies as a guiding spirit, God, listener and participant in this exercise.

The authority Augustine invokes supports what the French call an *idée–force*, a pivotal idea, the germ of an action. Merriam-Webster defines it as "an idea considered as a real factor in the behavior of an individual or social group and thus in the course of events." Original Sin is such an *idée–force*. Augustine's conclusion changed the way we view the human condition ever since. That children are born to repeat the dark behaviors of their forebears across generations is as old as the curse on the House of Atreus, or David sending Uriah the Hittite to death in battle so he might possess Bathsheba. But no one had made such a case as Augustine, linking the idea of his shameful personal act to the archetypal betrayal of God by the original parents from which we all are descended.

Locating the consequence of the Original Sin in his unoriginal sin, became the foundation of a theological system that occupied Augustine through his life. Was the idea already inherent in Augustine's act, like the oak in the acorn? Did the impulse to act grow from a deeper imperative to realize the latent idea?

Where does suffering come from...

Why is he still whispering to me as I write?

...and the guilt that calls it forth?

This is not an empty question. Words spill into it, and the form they take is a confession.

8 – *What Seymour Said*

Had Homer lived in the mid-20th Century, he might've found elements of his legacy updated in the writing of my old friend Seymour Krim, the father of Cultural Journalism. Seymour produced pioneering personal essays that propelled confessional writing into the post-modern world by marrying it to the uncompromising observations of a seasoned journalist with years of psychotherapy. He delivered these in the hair-trigger prose of a hit man on holiday handing out bouquets. In reality the vulnerability that peppered the page was his alone, and left the reader reluctant to blink. After listening to him read in the mid-70s, I sent him a note comparing his writing to the lit tip of a cigarette.

On August, 1989, at the age of sixty-seven, Seymour was found dead in his East10th Street apartment across from St. Mark's Church. His suicide from a drug overdose followed a debilitating heart attack and a deteriorating medical condition that would have made him dependent on the care of others. Seymour had lived alone in that one room for as long as I could remember, and such a prospect was intolerable to him. To paraphrase his suicide note, "I always knew the right time to leave a party."

Seymour wrote news articles, personal essays and profiles for the *Herald Tribune, The New Yorker, Swank, Nugget* and other alternative venues. But one has only to read his collections *Shake It for the World Smartass* (1970), and *You and Me* (1968), to understand the power of his voice. In his essay, "Notes Towards My Death," he notes "I don't think that I will die a 'natural' death because I am not sure there are any left," and speculates, wrongly, "Suicide is always a live possibility, although I have successfully fought off its lures all my adult life." His mother, he tells us, had jumped off a building in Washington Heights when he was ten. Perhaps what he anticipated accurately describes his demise seventeen years later. "My death, I believe, will be a meeting of the naked inner man with his true measure in a world of fatal fact."

Seymour's ability to frame a confession made a stolen pear seem more like a candy-apple. He transformed the convention launched by Augustine, and elaborated by Jean-Jaques Rosseau's *Confessions* (1782), and Thomas De Quincey's *Confession of an English Opium Eater* (1821), to one geared to the quickly changing post-modern world. The goal of writing for Seymour was the subject of his '50s essay, "The American Novel Made Me." He called it "the articulation of American reality by individuals who really, personally cared because their own beings were so helplessly involved in this newly-shifting, remarkably unstable, constantly self-analyzing and self-doubting society that had shot up after the war."

In this we hear the formal declaration of Cultural Journalism.

If he didn't originate the form, he certainly defined it. The approach called for the application of novelistic tools to historical events and notable people through the subjective lens of the writer, whose thoughts and feelings became an essential component of the narrative. Seymour championed the Beats, especially Kerouac, whose writing rang true to this definition. He cited the work of Norman Mailer, James Baldwin, Truman Capote, Joan Didion, and a succession of those who have extended this form.

There is a confessional heart beating at the center of Krim's finest writings. Cultural Journalist Vivian Gornick places "For My Brothers and Sisters in the Failure Business," on her list of *The Ten Greatest Essays, Ever* (2006). There is no more compelling *idée–force*, linked to personal disclosure, than what Seymour offers us in his exploration of the American Dream, what has shaped his enduring sense of failure: "…because I come from America, which has to be the classic, ultimate, then-they-broke-the-mold incubator of not knowing who you are until you find out. I have never really found out and I expect what remains of my life to be a long search party for the final me."

Even his footnotes, especially his footnotes, underpinned his text with a still deeper level of personal disclosure: "I think the time must come soon if mankind is going to find life possible when this romance with country has to be junked for the sake of everyone else. This world is made up of individuals—what my friend at the liquor store, Vinnie Porrazzo, calls God's children—not separate governments."

Vinnie, as a subatomic particle in this entanglement, is deeply personal and yet representative of the larger story because of the way Seymour frames it. His relationship to time, place, the very moment he captures, American culture in the New York '60s, demonstrates what Werner Heisenberg told us in his uncertainty principle, that the observer is inextricably bound to what is observed. This hybrid confession raises to visibility an interaction that is reciprocal and mysterious, but foundational to our world. The reader, entrained with the observer, becomes a participant in a narrative entanglement where particles in space not touching physically mirror each other over a distance.

9 – *Cultural Journalism*

Seymour Krim's essay, "The American Novel Made Me," published in *Playboy* in 1969, became the credo of Cultural Journalism. It elevated the personal narrative to a literary expression tailored to the speed and complexity of our time. As a boy, Seymour dreamed that to be a writer meant walking in the footsteps of Hemingway, John O'Hara and James M. Cain, those who "worked out their total hidden life before our eyes." The realistic novel had promised to reveal the mystery of the American soul, until TV, movies, and electronic media of every sort changed the culture. "These electronic whispers of tomorrow could in a momentary flash do what Flaubert and Conrad spent their lives trying to achieve with words: 'Above all, to make you see.'"

Seymour called upon the American writer to abandon the

"imitation or caricature" of reality, to replace the "mask of fiction" by going direct, to revolutionize the writer's relationship to the reader. The writer was to put his being on the page as he was on the telephone asking the reader a life-and-death question. Seymour moved the needle from the writer's act of confession to whomever might be listening, to placing the reader with him in the confessional; "due to what I have written our very lives will touch...your isolation or indifference has been penetrated by reading just as mine as by writing."

There is a Whitmanic ring to his vision reminiscent of *Song of Myself* where lives resonate to each other on a cellular level. Seymour understood that the road had changed from Whitman's time. Kerouac's road trip across America confirmed that it now carried busloads of alienated travelers to cities where jazz sessions in clubs and on street corners called forth soul from the shadows. For Seymour it became a "coast to coast restlessness" of zooming cars, blowing jazz solos and writing poems along the way. He addressed that restlessness and disconnection with the language forged in the furnace of improvisation, the confessional imperative of Cultural Journalism.

"You are there now, included in the network of my life as I am included in yours, and what you have seen and heard and identified...will not be put aside like a 'story' because it is an extension of the same reality that unites us both: I will have established a sense of community with you about the destiny of both our lives in this uncertain time..."

It is a curious irony that a writer who defined the mission, and wrote so powerfully in its behalf to express living history so powerfully should have fallen into almost total obscurity.

PART III – CUTTING THE CLOTH

10 - *Biographical Soul Speak*

For Swiss psychiatrist Carl Jung (1875-1961), the records and artifacts of civilizations could be read as a biography of the soul. From his perspective, Egyptian and Hermetic mysteries, the

Chaldean heavens. Greek view of Hades, the Gnostic speculations of Basilides, dream work from Asclepius to Freud, our image of God itself are all expressions of Psyche (soul) through the millennia. It isn't surprising that mid-way through life he started to work on what will become perhaps the unique outgrowth of his vision, *The Red Book*, which he describes as a confrontation with his unconscious. In terms of this discussion, Jung has deepened what began with Augustine as personal disclosure that moves us to confront timeless questions. to give us a biographical monument: Psyche Confesses Itself.

Jung broke from his increasingly acrimonious relationship with Sigmund Freud in 1913, after seven years of close association. He also withdrew from much of what had been a career on the ascent to re-evaluate his personal and professional path. During this time Jung withdrew to focus on his confrontation with his unconscious, recording it in a red leather bound folio. His most intense work on it spanned a period between 1913 and 1917, though he continued to add and revise until 1930.

The poetically driven prose rendered in illuminated Gothic script, features visionary encounters with mysterious figures in a psychological landscape. Many recognizable from history and myth, others with their own archetypal claims, insist on recognition as real rather than imagined entities. Pages of original artwork, figurative, and abstract, even today can be favorably compared to his contemporaries like Kandinsky, Feininger and Klee. Because Jung feared that the content would make him vulnerable to charges of being deranged, or just another *poète maudit* —do irreversible damage his reputation as a scientist—he withheld publication of what is clearly now the cornerstone of his life's work. It was finally published posthumously, with permission of his family, in 2009.

Following Jung into the landscape of the unconscious echoes Odysseus' encounter with the shades at the bloody trench at Erebus on his way back home. Jung crossed that threshold and descended into the Underworld to engage the figures he found there. In this respect, Jung emulated Dante's journey at the start of his Divine Comedy. Both found themselves mid-way through their lives shuddering at the entrance of dimensions beyond the range of normal experience, unable to turn back. Dante reads the inscription on the gate to the Underworld, *"Lasciate ogne speranza, voi ch'intrate*," most frequently translated, "Abandon all hope, ye who enter here." Jung is assailed as he crosses that threshold by an "unbearable inner longing" to call out: "My soul, where are you?"

Dante's soul-figure sends him Virgil as a guide.

In the process of pursuing his soul, Jung realizes he has forgotten her entirely. "I had to accept what I had previously called my soul was not at all my soul, but a dead system. Hence I had to speak to my soul as something far off and unknown, which did not exist through me, but through whom I existed."

*

The Red Book details Jung's journey to reconnect with the soul that calls to him from transpersonal inner depths rather than an external intellectual position in time. In finding his way through the personal unconscious with its traumas and conflicts, Jung discovered a deeper layer below it— an objective dimension he later identified as "the collective unconscious"—this encompassing psychological space where the shades of human history gather, well beyond personal disclosure.

James Hillman, in his commentary *Lament for the Dead, Psychology: After Jung's Red Book* (2013), points out that to engage the dead is to gather "the whole burden that the human being's soul carries." The task is to reanimate the wisdom of the ages, the soul lost to the self, and listen to what it has to say to us.

Jung, unlike Homer, didn't begin with the dead, but ended the Red Book with their appearance on his doorstep. In the first of the Seven Sermons to the Dead, he writes: "The dead came back from Jerusalem, where they found not what they sought. They prayed me let them in and besought my word, and thus I began my teaching."

In writing the The Red Book, the biography of his unconscious, Jung illuminated the structure and operation of psyche, the soul lost to itself, remembered. What followed this is a body of work that is perhaps one of the most comprehensive and profound explorations of the human condition any individual has left the world.

11 – *Biography of the Soul*

The idea is that in every life as it is lived, beneath the story we tell ourselves as we go, there is a deeper, unheard telling already taking place. Some hear the deep story partially, in moments of distraction or crisis, through dreams or epiphanies. Many, not at all. From this perspective, biographical writing, in all its forms, is a re-telling that reminds us to listen. The biographer, memoirist, confessor, cultural journalist is always in search of what breaks through the surface, unheard before this time, in pursuit of the soul.

Plato's dialogues are in their own right a form of biographical writing. Most obviously, his dialogues develop portraits of those around him, the conventions and details of Athens in the 4th Century BC. This is particularly true of his portrait of Socrates. At the start of the Symposium Socrates drifts away from the happy group he is with on the way to a banquet to hunker by the roadside as if in a trance. One of those familiar with this eccentric behavior explains to another who is not, that Socrates is listening to the inner voice that from time to time whispers in his ear. Socrates calls it his daemon, and has learned to honor it over the years. Getting drunk at the banquet, Alcibiades in his speech on love makes the point that although Socrates pretends to be attracted to young men, he, as the most beautiful of young men, was unable to seduce the old man who had become the object of his affection. In the course of the dialogues we get to know the full character of the man, as well as his ideas. We are dashed at the end when Socrates drinks hemlock as punishment for his conviction of bogus charge that he corrupted the youth and demeaned the gods of Athens. Crito had arranged for his escape on a ship waits not far outside the cell. Socrates' refusal to do so is final. His inner voice has told him that if he returns evil for evil, injustice for injustice, eventually even his friends will despise him. To flee and live comfortably in exile would undermine everything he has stood for. There is nothing to prove here. Plato has written a character study, a biography of the soul, and we grieve as Socrates swallows the poison that stops his heart.

Even in his most deeply philosophical dialogues, Plato the biographer uses the tools of the dramatist as Seymour Krim suggested the Cultural Journalist employ the novelist's craft to create intimacy. Seymour compared it to a telephone communication. We can hold the phone Plato hands us and hear Socrates voice on the other end of the line asking questions that we are tasked to answer. In the *Phaedrus*, Socrates asks: "But of the heaven which is above the heavens, what earthly poet ever did or ever will sing worthily?"

I would argue that in Plato, the philosophical and confessional impulses are opposites that work in tandem. Both strive to remember what has been forgotten, consistent with the Platonic theory of *anamnesis*, which states that learning is the recollection of what we already know.

It is the soul which must be remembered, "and such understanding is a recollection of those things which our souls beheld aforetime...looking down upon the things which now we supposed to be, and gazing up to that which truly is." (*Phaedrus*, 249)

"My soul, where are you?" cries Jung at the beginning of his journey.

Plato's work is as much psychological as it is philosophical. Philosophically, Materialists hold that mental states are products of the physical world, and Idealists the physical world a product of mind. Plato's philosophical dualism leap-frogs over this division by connecting the world of imperfect physical forms to archetypal forms of a transcendental mind—and validating the two as parts of a whole. This is the template of modern depth psychology.

Psyche/soul + logos/word system = psychology

Read this way, Plato's work is a biography of the soul, and the system that contains it— a psychology, or soul-system. This is true epic poems like the *Odyssey*, or the love story of Rama and Sita in the *Ramayana*, Dante's *Divina Comedia*, Nietzsche's *Zarathustra*, and Carl Jung's *Red Book*. The imperative at the heart of Biography is to let the soul, remembered, speak for itself.

12 – *Cracking the Code*

James Hillman talks about this lost and found again quality of the soul that unfolds biographically in his book, *The Soul's Code* (1997). He revisits Plato's myth of Er, at the end of the *Republic*, to talk about the pre-determined code of each soul as comparable to the oak in the acorn. Plato's dialogue describes the condition of souls in the after-world, in an account given by Er, a soldier thought to have died in battle, who revives five days later on his funeral pyre before it is set to the torch. He tells those present what he saw, the operation of the celestial spheres, and the protocols he witnessed for souls waiting on line to be reborn. Each was given a lottery token and an opportunity to choose his next life. Er saw a man who had been powerless in his last life choose to become a brutal dictator in the next one. Odysseus chose to be reborn as the son of a humble shopkeeper. In an orderly file, each soul passes three women at a long table working together: the Fates. Clotho spins the cloth, Lachesis allots the length, and the implacable Atropos cuts the cloth into which is woven the distinctive pattern of the soul's destiny. The pattern, or *paradegma*, is known to the soul, and the guardian spirit assigned to it. Before returning to the world, all souls must drink from the River of Forgetfulness, Lethe. Some, Er observes, drink more deeply than others. After remarking on this, Er finds himself, as if waking from a dream, on the funeral pyre.

The Romans referred to the soul's companion as the Genius, the inner voice. The Genius remembered the pattern of each soul, and whispered more audibly to some than to others. Those with whom it shared the secrets were empowered. Hence, what we have come to call a genius is someone who realizes the pattern in the weave, and fulfills his/her destiny.

Perhaps this is the mystery that drives all forms of biography. We listen for the genius whispering as we read, tune our ears to the whisper in ourselves. Prodigies, great artists and scientists, people who exhibit transcendent gifts, we speak of as having a calling. Hillman suggests that it is precisely that—they are gifted with a voice that calls loud enough to command attention, to demand it. Not a paltry whispering we eavesdrop on from time to time, but a shout, a slap, something that will not stand down.

13- *In conclusion*

In the First Century BC, the Roman poet Titus Lucretius Carus devoted the Sixth Book of his *De Rerum Natura* to the plague that devastated Athens in 420 BC, at the end of the second Peloponnesian War. The work focuses "on the nature of things," a world composed of atoms, sufficient unto itself, which required no metaphysical support from gods or an after-life. Lucretius argued that atoms, basic "particles," combining into complex structures, accounted for everything, including the universe where worlds like our own came and went. The soul that enabled our senses and cognition, also composed of atoms, dispersed when the body died. Nothing in nature endured, except the particles.

Lucretius dedicated the work to his friend Memmius, whom he hoped to persuade that death would hold no sting once he accepted the impermanence of all but the atoms that composed the world. He echoed his mentor Epicurus, who taught that freedom from superstition also freed one from the fear of death. Understanding our condition made it easier to let go of it.

The question arises, why did Lucretius end an argument geared to dispel fear with a horrific account of an event that occurred in Athens three hundred years earlier? The scenes of devastation he drew were so graphic, he might've been witnessing it firsthand.

> And whoso had survived that virulent flow
> Of the vile blood, yet into thews of him
> And into his joints and very genitals
> Would pass the old disease. And some there were,
> Dreading the doorways of destruction
> So much, lived on, deprived by the knife
> Of the male member; not a few, though lopped
> Of hands and feet, would yet persist in life,
> And some there were who lost their eyeballs: O
> So fierce a fear of death had fallen on them!

Not only the plague, but the brutal behavior between people with nothing to lose exposed the basic bottom line of their soul-less state. Such a display of unleashed suffering appears to have moved Lucretius from detached observer to fear filled creature. Steeped in impermanence, he may have been drawn to what he saw with his mind's eye, the plague inside of himself.

There were rumors that Lucretius has been the victim of a love potion, or written De Rerum Natura between periods of mental instability. The Roman poet died at forty-four, possibly a suicide. Nevertheless, he produced the most complete record of Epicurean thought, and its emphasis on freedom from fear through nonattachment. What Lucretius began as a biography of the physical world without reference to an enduring ontology, turned into a back-door biography of the soul.

   Biography is not only the act of writing about a life, but of life writing about itself.

   There has been an evolution of "biographical" forms in response to the changing culture. Memoir, Confession, Cultural Journalism, and variations of each including interfaces made possible by the technology that has given us hyper-text and virtuality. Even as we are prompted by the rhythms of our lives to be less emotionally connected, Biography can be more finely tuned to hear the inner whisper of the soul-system. Opposing the numbness of constant stimulation and short term gratification delivered by so many of the entertainments and distractions, a greater psychological awareness twinned by the sciences that connect the movements of subatomic particles to the stars moves us closer to the mystery of which we are composed. It is the same interconnectedness proposed by Thomas Lewis in his *Lives of a Cell*. The organelles he points out that exist within the cell as symbiotic forms not derived from the cell but support its existence may be analogized to Socrates' daemon, the Genius that accompanies the soul into a life in time, remembers the individual paradigm and whispers to it from the depths. The voice Jung calls the "spirit of the depths" prompts him to risk descending into the unknown in himself to later bring to light a Biography of the Soul as he experiences it: 'You are an image of the unending world, all the last mysteries of becoming and passing away live in you.'"

BIBLIOGRAPHY:

AUGUSTINE, of Hippo, *The Confessions of St. Augustine*, Forgotten Books, 2016

DERRIDA, Jacques, *Disseminations*, tr. Barbara Johnson, Chicago, University of Chicago Press, 1983

HILLMAN, James,
_____*Re-Visioning Psychology*, New York, Harper Paperbacks, 1977
_____ *The Soul's Code, In Search of Character and Calling*, New York, Grand Central Publishing, 1997
_____*Lament of the Dead, Psychology after Jung's RED BOOK*, with Sonu Shamandasani, NY, W.W. Norton, 2013

KRIM, Seymour,
_____*Shake it for the World, Smartass*, New York, A Delta Book, 1970
_____*You & Me*, New York, Holt, Rinehart and Winston, 1974

ROUSSEAU, Jean-Jacques, *Confessions*, New York, Oxford University Press, 2000

HOLLIS, James, *Mythologems, Incarnations of the Invisible World*, Toronto, Inner City Books, 2004

JUNG, C.G. *The Collected Works*, (Bollingen Series XX) 20 vol. Trans. R.C.F. Hull. Ed. H. Read, Princeton University Press, 1953-79
_____*Man and his Symbols*, New York Doubleday and Co;, 1964
_____*Memories, Dreams, Reflection*, Ed. Aniela Jaffe, New York, Pantheon Books, 1961
_____*The Red Book; Liber Novus*, Edited and introduced by Sonu Shamandasani. New York, W.W. Norton, 2009

JUNG, C.G., and Wolfgang PAULI, *Atom and Archetype: The Pauli-Jung Letters* 1932-1958, Edited by C.A. Meier, Princeton NJ; Princeton University Press, 2001

NIETZSCHE Friedrich, *The Portable Nietzsche*, Ed. Walter Kaufman, New York, Viking, 1972

PEAT, F. David. *Synchronicity: The Bridge Between Matter and Mind*, New York: Bantam, 1987
_____*Infinite Potential, The Life and Times of David Bohm*, MASS., Addison-Wesley, 1997

PINES, Paul, *My Brother's Madness*, Curbstone Press, CT 2007

PLATO,
_____*Plato's Phaedrus*, ed. R. Hackforth, NY, The Library of the Liberal Arts, 1952
_____*Five Great Dialogues*, ed. L. Loomis, Walter J.Black, Inc. NY 1942

RUPESTRIAN Z,E(A),M,I,-VERSE

Jesse Glass

oh my Question in the Sky!

the Wounded Hand

oh my birth mark signed & counter-signed by a Memling anguipede!

the Hand the Wound the Hand the Wound the Hand

a Continent of Anthropophagi!

to be Wept to be Wept to be Wept

oh my Interstellar Ice Block!

the Hand the Wound the Hand

a M,i,t,e, traversed it/ Tardigrade hopped it

to be Wept to be Wept to be Wept to be Wept to be Wept

the L,i,g,h,t, crushed big bang orts & needles reverberating 'cash
cash' Thru It

the Hand the Wound the Hand the Wound

a Vespiary of Silver Excitations

to be Wept to be Wept to be Wept

The Stone that shatters into 18 equal portions when expertly spat
upon

the Hand the Wound the Hand the Wound the Hand

Sentient Molecule!

To be Wept to be Wept to be Wept to be Wept

Sound of a winded Horse///Sound of written Water///sound of a giddy
gong

[MUSICAL INTERLUDE]

the Hand the Wound the Hand the Wound

Ass-Headed Magician!

To be Wept to be Wept to be Wept

Forehead of Evacuated Space

the Hand the Wound the Hand the Wound the Hand

oh my L,e,p,e,r, L,i,o,n!

the Wounded Hand

A,n,t, into E,l,e,p,h,a,n,t,

to be Wept to be Wept to be Wept

E,l,e,p,h,a,n,t, into A,n,t,

the Hand the Wound the Hand the Wound the Hand

Yelp of a Fox turned blood & fur by Hounds

the Wounded Hand

that Decussated Cry

to be Wept to be Wept to be Wept

we climb to the top of the Fragrantest Tree in the East

the Hand the Wound the Hand the Wound

the moon's martial C,o,o,t,e,r, above the clouds

to be Wept to be Wept to be Wept

a Fallopian Harp--prepared with Pegs and Dampers

the Hand the Wound the Hand the Wound the Hand

mounted on crystal gimbals

to be Wept to be Wept to be Wept

Oh my Highway of Scar Tissue

the Hand the Wound the Hand the Wound

C,a,l,i,p,e,r,s, structuring the ever-welling V,o,i,d,

to be Wept to be Wept to be Wept

Oh my Mathematic Gloom!

The Hand the Wound the Hand

Flies punishing the Face

To be Wept to be Wept to be Wept to be Wept

O Clapperclaw, cry Clapperclaw, lo Clapperclaw!

the Hand the Wound the Hand the Wound the Hand

the embowered Crab embedded in lower lip, left cheek

to be Wept to be Wept to be Wept

[MUSICAL INTERLUDE]

mourn
like a ball-bearing
drips oil & light

!

like a slab of oak
planed but not sanded,
darkens

!

mourn
like a wide-mouthed jar
set out all night
in a storm

from minn*mouth:*
a collection of tide*poems* in the languages
of the East coast of the British isles,
from Shetland to Suffolk

Alec Finlay

DEDICATED TO THE MEMORY OF BILL GRIFFITHS (1948–2007)

EY, AY, OY: ISLAND
EIÐ: ISTHMUS
EÁ: STREAM
EYRR: SAND OR GRAVEL STRAND
ÁL: EEL
STRAUMR: CURRENT
OSS: RIVER MOUTH

BUNGAY   BINGISLE

bill   bing

he do   he do

bend a bow   heap a pile

EYE   ISLED

                    see
             there aint
          no tides –
     wot th <u>Doves</u>
   happd beck-
  ards round
    wusn is   land
        keepnis nose
          n eyes owt
                 th slubby

STROMA   STRUMMER
STROMFIRTH   STREAMFORTH

ða strummerbeuys   beateen time onða
        inða harbor   quoy oweranower

EYEMOUTH   STREAMOUTH
AIRS   STRANDS

ða ballage o peebel-een   gliskit atill ða loomie

da skyrin faain   dimmer atill da
blind stonns oða eager
          makina dim bore
          ða fēger nusts in
                 everra evenin   dwynan   an swinan

atill ða blu nichtide

or whelmed   atill ða whaal

EDAY   NECKISLE

a bar fir aaða in-atween-

ers tae haal fae   drinktaedrink

FIDRA   FEATHERY ISLE

ane meikle licht cleaves   th derk frith   an glists

aroad fir fedders   blawn toanfrae   spital walls

AUBURN   EELBURN

wotzat rinnin ina gleam

inter

th sweel

writhin froom th keld

oar trappit   inter split light

inder wettor-

hyel?

THE OYCE   THE PUSS

"loss ma voyce"   (the river whispers to the sea)

"yi cheust hae tae rowl wi it"   (the sea calls back)

YARMOUTH   BURBLERIVER MAW

unna   tina   wether   unna   tina   wether   unna   tina   wether

countin a power shinin pitals   spins wer eyes

   inta th draw yaw o   th blowin windflars

      whose masts   ha th task o

         hemmn th searoad n

         anchoren th vista o

         th triqutera era

ENGLISH

Bungay (for Alistair Peebles)

bill, he bends a bow; bing, he heaps a pile

Eye

see, there aren't any tides [here] – what the River Dove is wrapped
backwards around was, and is, land, keeping its nose and eyes out of the
mud

Stroma (for Hanna Tuulikki)
Stromfirth

the strummer boy in the harbour is beating time on the quay, over and over

Eyemouth
Airs, Ayres (for Robert Alan Jamieson)

the ballast of the pebble-eye, glimpses through the mist – the shimmering
sky becomes dimmer in the little light – or nap – of the stones, as the tide
makes a small opening in the dimness, which the sun nests inside every
evening, dwindling and wasting away, until it has sunk into the blue tide of
night, or submerged itself in the belly of a whale

Eday (for Neil Firth)

a bar (or isthmus) for all the in-betweeners to haul [their boat] from drink to drink (sea to sea)

Fidra

one great light cleaves the dark and shines a road for feathers blown to and from the hospice walls

Auburn

what's that running in a gleam – into the swell, writhing from the smooth water, into the turning tide (sparkling), or trapped in the rockpool?

The Oyce

lost my voice… (the river whispers to the sea); you just have to roll with it (the sea calls back)

Yarmouth

one two three: counting the many shining petals out to sea spins our eyes into the slow oscillation of these blooming windflowers [windmill turbines], whose masts have the task of holding back the sea-road, and anchoring the vista of the triquetera era

Notes

Bungay (TM 335895): village in a bend of River Waveney, *Waggly River,* which formed a barrier between Norfolk and Suffolk. As with Eye, **ay** refers to a peninsula. **Bingr**, ON, heap or pile; **bing**, Sc, heap of mining spoil. **Hap**, Nor, wrap, cover. As an alternative Briggs and Kilpatrick suggest *Island in the Bend*, from OE **buging**; and David Mills gives *Island Settlement of Buna's People.*

Eye (TM 145735): market town at the confluence of River Dove and a tributary; **ey**, from **eg**, OE and ON, **ig**, AS, island, peninsula, or land surrounded by marsh or river – which this would once have been. Also **Ig,** AS, related to **ea**, stream, from **å**, ON, river, stream. Other Suffolk examples include Bawdsey, Kirsey, and Lindsey. Island is Ø in Danish, Ö in Swedish. **Beckards**, Suff, backwards; **slubby**, Suff, muddy.
Stroma (ND 353792): abandoned island in the Pentland Firth; the name means *Isle of the Stream*; **straumr**, ON, **strøm**, Da, **ström**, Sw, stream, from PIE ***sreu-**, to flow. **Ey**, ON, island. **Inða, onða**, Sc, in the, on the. **Quoy,**

OrN, quay. Stromfirth (HU 404500): farm by Loch of Strom, Shetland, also from **straumr**, stream, current.

Eyemouth (NT 945645): Berwickshire coastal village; from **eá**, OE, stream. Airs, Ayres (HU 342571): now Ayres, township, by Aith Voe, Shetland; from **eyrr**, sand, gravel, or pebbles by water, usually alluvium at the mouth of a burn. It occurs in other Shetland place-names as **ør**, also common in Sogn, Norway. The poem mixes Shetlandic and Northumbrian. **Ballage**, Sh, ballast (stones). **Peebel**, Sc., pebble, **chingle** in Orkney. **Gliskit**, Sh, glimpsed (of sunshine); **atill ða**, Sh, in, within the. **Loomie**, North, looming, hazy appearance of land towards the horizon. **Skyrin**, Sh, **skyelly**, OrN, **skimmer**, Nor, covering of bright, glittering clouds with a glamsy appearance, from **skjell**, N, clear, visible, transparent. **Dimmer**, Sh, darken, dusk, twilight; **faa**, Sh, fall; **blind**, Sh, a little light, short nap, to close the eyes (in sleep); also, dark, obscure; **stonn**, Sh, stone. **Eagre,** North, tidal bore. **Bore**, Sh, small opening; **fēger**, Sh, sun; **nust, noust**, Sh, OrN, dry dock for a boat. **Dwynan, dwine**, Sc, North, decline, dwindle, from **swinan**, OE, waste away. **Whelmed**, submerged, from **hweielfan**, OE, to cover. **Whaal**, Sh whale; '*inside the whale*' is given as one of the answers to the question *where does the sun shine at night?*, in 'Adrian and Ritheus', quoted in Bill Griffiths *Anglo-Saxon Magic*.

Eday (HY 560341): island named for its isthmus, from **eið**, ON, isthmus, ***h₁y-**, PIE, to go, and **Oy**, ON, island, with the same meaning as the Suffolk Eye. The isthmus connects Loch of Doomy and Bay of London, from **lund-inn**, N, woodland. **Fae**, Sc, from. Oluf Rygh *gives eið as 'a small piece of land linking two broader strips, and of a deep indentation in a hill, which affords an easier route between two rural districts...'* Doreen Waugh notes the importance of such isthmus to communication, commerce, and portage. EMEC conduct tidal energy research at Fall of Warness, Eday.

Fidra (NT512868): one of the small isles of the Firth of Forth. *Fether-ay*, from **fiðra**, ON, feather, giving *feather isle*, for its seabird colonies, though William Patterson says this is a folk etymology, preferring *fuð*, ON, cleft, split – a fanny but in a less feathery way. There is a Stevenson lighthouse and ruins of a Cistercian **lanzaretto**, quarantine hospital – Sc, **spital** – for sailors. **Meikle, muckle**, Sc, big, great; **frith**, Sc, firth; **glist**, Sc, shine; **fedder**, Sc, feather.

Auburn (TA 169627): coastal village in East Riding, abandoned because of erosion. Rather than the colour, it derives from **eel**, stream, from OldScand **ál**. Francesco Perono Cacciafoco gives the root ***alb-**, from PIE ***al-**, feed, nourish, connected to ***albh-**, water, currents, rain, shining water, white, and the Germanic name of the eel, **aal**. Fish was introduced into the human diet during the Upper Paleolithic. **Split,** North, turn of the tide; **keld**, North, smooth stretch of water, from **kelda**, ON, deep smooth water; **inta**, North, into the; **wettor-hyel**, North, rockpool, collected by Katrina Porteous.

The Oyce (HY 288298): burn flowing from <u>Loch of Swannay</u>, to the sea, near <u>Costa</u>, <u>Orkney</u>, from **óss**, ON, river or burn mouth. **Rowl**, Sc, roll.

Yarmouth (TG 527065): locals never refer to 'Great' in the name of this Norfolk harbour-town. **Yare**, OE **gerne**, from the Celtic root, **ger**, **gar**, babbling river. Norfolk is the most northerly of the Southern Dialects of <u>England</u>. Trudgill quotes Claxton's *Suffolk Dialect*, which records local shepherds using a numerical system that bore traces of Brittonic as late as the 19th c: **unna**, **tinna**, **wethder**, **tether**, **pinkie**, Suff, one, two, three, four, five; **un**, **tri**, W, one, three; **pump**, W, five; **dick**, Suff, **deg**, W, ten. **Pitals**, Nor, petals; **draw**, Nor, move slowly; **power**, Nor, a great number; **blow**, Nor, blossom; **hemmn**, Nor, hemming. **Sea-roads**, from AS **hron-rad**, *the whale road*, and locally, <u>Yarmouth Roads</u>. Forby gives an <u>East Anglian</u> use of **anchor** for tree roots, which '*anchor out*'. **Yaw**, oscillation around an axis of wings or blades. **Triquetra**: symmetrical triangular ornament of three interlaced arcs, a motif fitting for the windmill turbine, symbolic of the array of 30 offshore windmills at <u>Scroby Sands</u>, installed in shallow water near the port.

tidal poetics

Alec Finlay

'*The poet's justification is the richness of his vocabulary.*'

– *Sadok sudei II*, A Trap for Judges II, Russian Futurist manifesto , 1913, D. Buriuk, E. Gure, N. Buriuk, V. Maiakovskii, E. Nizon, V. Khlebnikov, B. Livchits, A. Kruchenykh

The sea is, once again, a theme for our time. Our relationship to the coast is changing. Minn*mouth* bodes the threat of coastal inundation and promise of marine renewables. The poems are anchored by place-names; they utlize the regional languages of the East Coast of the British Isles, from the Out Stack of Unst to Great Yarmouth. These include Orkney and Shetland Norn c.1800, recorded in the classic dictionaries of Jakobsen, Marwick, Stout Angus, and Graham, and, traveling down the coast, the *Dictionar o the Scots Leid* (*Dictionary of the Scottish Language*), and records of English regional languages, including Forby's *The Vocabulary of East Anglia,* and Bill Griffiths anthology *Fishing and Folk.*

Russian Futurist or will*beist* poets referred to themselves as word*makers*; I have proposed wave*wright* and wind*wright* to refer to designers of energy devices, and speech*wright,* for makars who follow the precepts of tidal*poetics.* Minn*mouth* riffs off Futurist poetics, especially the inspired word*maker* Velimir Khlebnikov, who grew up by the Caspian Sea among the Kalmyk people, '*Mongol nomads of a Buddhist faith*'. Markov explains that '*the sounds of foreign tongues*' marked his poetry in terms of sense and sound: this project follows Khlebnikov's use of neologisms, dialect, and ancient languages.

The minn*mouth* poems flow from elements of place-names and are composed in a phonetic synthesis of contemporary speech, creating a potential vocabulary that exceeds conventional orthography and aspires to become a resource for offshore technology. As Vahni Capildeo says, there are still people who think they have no accent: their speech may have a grip on power, but it lacks energy.

I would like to thank Harry Giles, Katrina Porteous, Ian Duhig, Peter Trudgill, Alistair Peebles, William Patterson, Laura Watts, and Ken Cockburn for their guidance in terms of Orkney Norn, Scots (from Caithness to Berwick), Northumbrian, Yorkshire, East Anglian, and Danish words and names.

AF
Newhaven, *Newharbour*

Yinglossia

Ariel Resnikoff

& I shld know as little about it as I do   this substance   . . . aheym . . .
*   the people of substance   for a change   turn the radio station*
to the "old days" [lit. years of sobyetski]   when money swirled the drain
*   & nobody complained   in the middle of the night [lit. at the hour of study]*
a sour odor   filled the cafeteria; a stink [lit. rot]   bad breath [lit. a putrid tongue]

Prologue

he is talking nonsense

is he bewildered? [lit. taboo]

he eats as if recuperating from illness

he is making a mess

he eats like a horse

he is thick-headed in fog

he is squirming in horseradish

perhaps he has a cold? [lit. malaria (ague) is all he gets]

he has nothing

he has nothing at all [lit. an itch or boil]

only strange practices

odd ways

no say [lit. power]

a man who criticizes non-existence [lit. climbs up walls]

he creeps like a bed-bug

doesn't know where to look

he is blind [lit. rhetorical]

ruins the language

the violent stutterer

talks into the world

he talks into sickness

talks into restlessness [lit. pins or needles]

he is only good for fowl sacrifice [lit. worthless]

he shd go to hell

he shd meet w/ korach's death [lit. the earth swallow him]

he is a shame to our children

he is nothing at all

**out of which the following plan occurred [lit. standing on one leg]

it never happened!

he never was [lit. speaking in tongues]   there

still is

as in: it is not worth a knock of earth

as in: it is very cheap [lit. impossibly expensive]

the nonsense speech [lit. deformed tongue]
                                cd be
                                        it doesn't matter
it is not becoming [lit. doesn't fit]
                       it fits like a slap in the face
                              it is the voice of a false-messiah [lit. sarcasm]
it hurts me
           he appears to me
                       he is fainting [lit. emptied]
nothing will help
                it will help like blood-cupping on a corpse
                                       it will do
it will have to
             will it heal in time for the wedding?
                              it must
no matter
           let us eat & be healthy

Firstspeech

praise god! thanks & pray. recite the 18 benedictions. *vo den* (cut-off [lit: what else])? no sweat. god [lit. the name] respects the humble somebody -- does he? berates the evil-ones (may they choke on their tongues [lit. languages]). the real article is a bargain for hire. the chew-among-chews. for rent or (re)lease. it pleases me, see? my heart told me so, see? i predicted it, see? likewise: keep it moving! don't bother me [lit. don't throw a hook around my nose]! **a stutterer was seen as a scatterbrain, confuser, & somehow also a conniver, twister, self-promoter, not to be trusted [lit. jew] human dung was attributed to [lit. the inferior merchandise]. now we talk excessively or not at all. a groan, maybe even a disparaging sigh, cd be: lies on the square & still talking non-sense

Friendlyface

friendly face. that familiar face.
like a hot bath. like a bowl of chopped meat.
stop banging on my head [lit. bargaining w/ my sanity]
the gargling solution shd be
fresh breath? o, that it shld come true! who bringeth forth bread from
the earth, etc.
to the common people, for a bargain say, not only to do business
but for heartache, see? sweetheart (singing) *my heart's love
is a pit in the earth . . .*
listen: you can shake-stammer
in impending fire
from stuffed cabbage to stuffed cabbage to
(*holebshes/holishkes/holubtshe*) depending on
from-where --
& so I made a mistake, so the words abrade, so what?
i've been called worse than debauchee
many times before, a cain-raiser
carouser, mad man, mongrel, kyke --

Downtheoldhatch

for LZ

i.

down the old hatch, skol! -- & up my white mouth, onto bib, fringed
scrap covered mist [lit. refuse]; I was spewing litvish "funereal"
shrewdness against the wall: a black [lit. singed] magic transcription
[lit. false-messiah]

ii.

which one arrives at when one has no business left to tend
-- no trade, calling, nor income -- when one is forced to live by
improvisation alone, drawing livelihood "from the air" -- & not
achieving anything, but starving by our wits

iii.

come to the point
[lit. make it sharp]

scream like hell
[lit. spill yr guts]

curse the name
[lit. ruin yrself]

> --what's the difference? [lit. as typically recited by the youngest child]

Lizardslaugh

**the expert-connoisseur know-it-all brings a boil from the cut "crippled-tongue" to the inspector-overseer of kashrus:

it's my own fault, I know [lit. I cooked it]. might vomit from the smell of it, but can't get rid of it . . .

it's delicious [lit. the lizards laugh] -- they don't let you live!

talk & talk & talk yr tongue off! it is said that a jew who works on the sabbath [lit. an invalid] is not fit to suck a ham. the long meaningless rigmarole [slang, lit. scroll of esther] implanted in my speech --

o forget it! you're nothing more than a derelict nibbler [lit. sweet tooth]:

(singing) *sweetheart darling child in me -- sweet little soul in me --* what difference does it make whether we live or die? the inf(l)ected tongue -- may it keep its distance! & the impure food [slang, lit. pig feed] doesn't do a thing. not today & not tomorrow [lit. never after the closing prayer], but out of thin air hangs on. now only god knows . . . so? well? move it along already! hurry up! aren't you gone yet?

Mincha

for Anne Tardos

in praise & submission to a baby-son [yiddishism (derisive)] -- let
us prepare the tools for extraction [lit. from tongues]. if the fever
is of a jewish head -- is it a shaygets luck? There's no evil eye,
either way, as they say *(tu-tu)*, the canary keep away. single men of
marriageable age [lit. little birds] crippled into misfits for a spoiled lap
of milk, narrowly achieved [lit. hardly lived to see] the transformation
of soars into sacrifice (slang [lit. false-messianism]). raw groats
(a mess-up [lit. mix-up of]) & cooked groats w/ broad noodles at
a kosher boarding-house-cafeteria in the far-reaches of the bronx
[lit. a lively russian dance, usually to a sexual cause (ie. of 'blind
mixing')]. an amulet [lit. charm, (from german, "*kind-bet-tzettel*")] worn
at birth, containing psalm 121: *di nomen fun melokhim* [lit. names
of angels] -- envision a god in labor, & after, old & young, eating
plates of stuffed derma (in flour & onion, salt, feffer & shmaltz, (to
keep them in skins) -- the ticklish little prigs (technically, talkative
little jews [lit. fruitless idle questions)]: not in "reality," so to say [lit.
"as if it *were*" (pronounced *ver*)], round dumplings made of groat-
meal cooked-up in pork-belly stew & tied at the corners in 'bakers
handkerchiefs.' dumplings filled w/ potatoes & livers, kidneys & barley
at a kosher boarding-house-cafeteria on the bronx grand concourse.
for a petulant excitability by a gad-about gang of jews gathers about:
"he had been perfect [lit. legitimate] before the cross-eyed sickness
took!" first in small pockets of dough filled w/ meat & curd-cheese, the
magic-worker, trickster, phony casper milquetoast corrupts the root-
canals of the pure jewish jaw. a virus of the tongue & teeth [lit. cheek
& mouth] -- how does it infect? **in force of false laughter & aguish
[lit. idling], the loafer lox-addict stutterer stumbles out of the afternoon
prayer-hall wreathing in false thanks & praise: "may we fan forever the
shekhinah embers"! [lit. blessed is the vessel as it breaks]

Blessedarewe

go away! go hump w/ the whales (peddle yr fish elsewhere [lit. whistle
at a leviathan]).
go to hell [lit. may you choke on yr tongue]! shit in the ocean. spill yr
guts.
spill yr guts against the city hall.
spill yr guts against the synagogue [lit. house-of-entry]
that you shd threaten the "holy geese" upon entering (& don't frighten
me [lit. you little non-native jew of galicia])!
someone hollers: go frig yrself . . .
the same to you! [hebraism, lit. big deal... (derisive)]
tho it doesn't turn-out the way we planned. there is no "complete man"
to bribe, see? blessed are we, w/ children & all (in fractured english
[lit. utter
misery]), we are chopped in w/ the herring & vodka [lit. minced]

Firstburial

i'm dying for it [lit. my soul expiring] -- that delicacy called "bad taste."
as an old mumbling hebrew teacher is w/out his *heder* [lit. one-room
school] -- i am called unpalatable [lit. soured] & accused of crazy fowl
chatter-cracklings. called crazy kyke & sold from house to house [lit.
kosherly butchered] at a bargain

for as the light said unto me, unto you there shall be a tiny box
henceforth containing 2 tiny portions of deuteronomy (vi. 4-9 & xi 13-
2') lines handwritten on a goatskin parchment in 22 tongues

it doesn't frighten me, see? i'm not having it, see?
& perhaps on account of the indoor bath they call *mikve* or what?
a dietary constraint that cuts between food?
or what?
yr cutlery kept separate?
or what?
a quorum of men holding worship?
or what?

try harder! recite the 18 prayers!
or what?
one way or (an)other.
w/out promise [lit untruthfully] speaking in

Rebitsn//Rebbe

he who "compassions mercy": rabbi, mister rabbi, *dear . . !* (it was the
rabbi's wife's almost sarcastically over-pious [lit. to shout & get no
answer] whispering thru the slats: "for all the good it'll do ya --"

the inflammatory sickness starts
in the mouth & works it's way up. doesn't bother w/ ious. pays cash in
advance.

o god in heaven, master of the uni-verse -- who knows if he's the real
mccoy...*!* this "nervous" body talking non-sense cd just as soon be
acting-out a part

as be that he who "goes to the devil" [lit. speaks in tongues] -- a tooth
into his mother's toe ! or do I mis-speak? they call me violent names
"in a language of rags" : "the wandering kyke" -- *bite yr tongue!*

Commonsense

what a..*!* what kind of a..*!* what's it matter to you, *huh*? now don't get
excited [lit. burst into flame]. it stinks -- what'r you talking? smack
smack (gently said) wd you keep quiet? (shouted) quiet, I said,
shutup! there's the professional (professorial) type who makes a living
from it, gathering these pious sheep, berating the irreligious (who
"flout" the sacred law. "beautiful as the seven worlds," (belles lettres,
& w/ a hearty laugh [lit. half-sarcastically]). the wig at the wedding
she wore ever after (was a watchword greeting, beadle at the *shtibl*
quoting old policeman's slang: "it had been a brothel whorehouse
(before) mix of wool & linen"). now you oughta be ashamed of
yrself [lit. to the bottom of yr throat]. the prettier ones they bury [lit.
this one is an ugly one]. & gather pleasure, the little nothings for

a "messenger drunkard" -- non-jewish [lit. impious or wild one]. or
if to skin one, a hag-mare worthless one [lit. mischievous child] or
apoplectic wreck. where the customer is king [Americanism], a snake
can also be a shrew clumsy bungler, drag, poor, luckless sponger,
butter-fingered shmock

Behindtheschola

**quick quickly, the beggar watchman elijah cuts young mens' pious at
an all-time-low:
"now cut it short!"
have you finished the dirty work?
pins & needles in his toe (a spanking-new proverb preaching another
wretched thing:
just think how it reflects
on the religious
democracy!) the very rich [lit. stone rich] strong & brave, shitting sorrel
grass soup -- piece-pits in a leafy green stew (yiddishism,

> idiomatic for those inclined to
> heretics: "one who becomes dumb
> like a piece of wood" [lit. loses
> speech])

-- tell the children ('s children! some fool. a bit of piece tricks the
smaller bits toward quiet death. prideful sweet-cakes in skin-thin
dough rolled-up
in blue cheese & rotted beef. a push-shove vulgarism or *vilde khaye*
[lit. wild beast] behind the *schola* in a snored aside:
a bent new year !   it's gone -- it doesn't matter. the sour
cream's always already & sour. finally (pronounced *phew*)! listen --
hold on -- how's this

Parvenu

so now, get rid of it:
alas for alack, woe unto *whom?*
either too much or too little [lit. a wallop or a toot]
"dear me!" (imitatingly -- *parvenu!*
cut it short [lit. w/out intro(duction)]
conceited & peevish
sulky & stuffed in a puffy shirt
or tired-out
& sputtered as confused
little pups [lit. overly made-up]
"the rich are too stuffed-up
to photograph" [lit. stuffed in dead birds]
& drunk
me bothersome hanger-on
cursing in
disorderly
survival

Author's Note

Ariel Resnikoff

I arrive at the present work thru a practice of translingual-poetic (translational) deformance across/between multiple code-switching dialects. My compositional method traverses by (mis) translation in/to Yiddish-, Hebrew- & Aramaic-English, the adapted sonic/semantic properties of these grammars, syntaxes & lexicons, & takes English as its temporary "host," while performing perpetual inflectional slippages—interlingual punning & fusion-slangs, as much as the host can absorb.

The dybbuk (Yiddish: spirit-possessor), which my Jewish-Ashkenazi ancestors believed to inhabit the body of the wild stutterer, mad person, heretic or *"akher"* [lit. other], became the peripheral focus of this poetry. I began to imagine the "odd" transgressional practices of that other(ed) marginal antinomian ancestor —the "possessed"— & to consider the ways in which this "possession" *by* language might manifest in my own "odd" practices, which so mark me as poet, translator and jew. I use the word "odd" here in deliberate echo of the terms against which Sabbatean stigma was transcribed in 17th-century Palestine: "for the odd practices of a false messiah."

In which La Nature rejects its correlates

(after Baudelaire's Correspondances)

Robert Mittenthal

"Self-revelation is annihilation of self"

Lana Turner's living
Still life of words
(see baud rate, see disambiguation)
You lost me at Shirley
Temple's temple
Mounts of words
Crossed forests
Crossed out
Intimate symbol
Of sweets
Of the stink
Of subjects she sings

No man's mottled nose
No oboe
to judge
to Cleave amber

Nature is never adequate
to the revolting dead
Adolescent
Hardwood doubled
Green screened
Vibrant bullet
Organized
as if subjects exist

Not knowing it's dead
La fabrique du pre
Works day and night
Green light for white flight
As it reproduces itself
Say what?
Delete stink of flesh
Deep aura
Echo as ecstasy
Connotes
'Heads up!'
No cognate released
No sense of singing
Vampire blood on lip
No scent of infinite thing
Gasping abreast

"Shall two know the same in their knowing?"

Ian Brinton

In Canto 93 from *Section: Rock-Drill* Pound quotes Dante's *Convivio*

"quest' unire
"quale è dentro l'anima
Veggendo di fuori quelli che ama"

and in his *Companion to the Cantos* Carroll F. Terrell translated these lines as "And this union [is what we call love, whereby we can know] what is inside the mind by seeing outside the thing it loves". The words in brackets are left out by Pound. The next word in the Canto is "Risplende" standing in a line on its own, shining, before the poet emphasises the centrality of presence, "Manifest and not abstract". I think that when Michael Grant and I decided to embark upon some collaborative translations of poetry from the French originals we firmly held in mind that sense of presence: something made 'Manifest'.

Our earliest collaborations arose from looking at the poems of Yves Bonnefoy and we published two small volumes of these with Oystercatcher Press run by Peter Hughes, a noted translator of both Petrarch and Cavalcanti. In Bonnefoy's 1976 essay, "The Translation of Poetry", he proposed that poetry, "the very thing we cannot grasp or hold", is the very thing we can translate, because, unlike the fixed nature of the poem itself, the poetry is unfixed. A translation is poetry re-begun and we should try to relive the act that produced the poem. It is as if the translator must aim to renew that impulse to bridge the *dentro* to the *veggendo*. However, whereas a material bridge is passive and inert we felt that our translations must attempt to make a construction of energy with which to convey the active experience of a foreign original text. We also took heed of Bonnefoy's warning about the unimaginative bondage of the translator who becomes a hostage to words; we did not wish to cripple the experience through bondage to a text. We felt that we had to proceed with caution: the ontological rightness of our newfound images mattered much more than whether they matched term by term, in a skin-deep resemblance, those of the original.

After our versions of Bonnefoy we decided to look at Mallarmé and adopted a similar pattern of working. Michael would write a first draft which was a close approximation to a literal translation and we then used this as our skeleton. In response I would then re-write the poem accompanying changes with a little comment as to why I felt that these changes were appropriate. In a sense this became a little like an act of close textual criticism. We would then meet up and put together a final version for publication. What now follows is the original French sonnet 'SALUT' and the two versions that Michael Grant and I put together:

> Rien, cette écume, vierge vers
> A ne désigner que la coupe;
> Telle loin se noie une troupe
> De sirènes mainte à l'envers.

> Nous naviguons, ô mes divers
> Amis, moi déjà sur la poupe
> Vous l'avant fastueux qui coupe
> Le flot de foudres et d'hivers;

> Une ivresse belle m'engage
> Sans craindre même son tangage
> De porter debout ce salut

Solitude, récif, étoile
A n'importe ce qui valut
Le blanc souci de notre toile.

The following first draft is the version which Michael sent to
me, titled 'TOAST', and we worked from that:

Nothing, this foam, pure verse
Referring only to the cup;
So drowns a distant troupe
Of sirens, most of them head first.

We sail on, my various friends,
Me on the poop already,
You at the ornate prow that cuts
The wave of thunderbolts and winters;

A superb drunkenness urges me
To be unafraid even of the pitching
And propose this toast on my feet

To solitude, reef, star
And whatever else was worth
Our sail's blank consideration.

My first response to this was to question the use of the word
'cup'. I suggested that surely 'la coupe' referred to the external form
of the poem, the structure within which the words can be contained.
This raised the stakes a bit and so we opted for 'chalice' instead. I
wasn't altogether happy with the word 'distant' in line 3; it seemed
to me that 'loin' was further away than that: 'far-off' into the distance
perhaps. We also mischievously contemplated the phrase 'down the
hatch' as perhaps being not altogether inappropriate in a poem that
is titled 'Salut'! More importantly we discussed the sense that the
poem was about the poet as Odysseus and that this should inform
the language of our translation. This led to 'friends' becoming 'crew'
and the poet 'lashed' to the mast as the Greek hero passed the
island of the Sirens. Some of the changes we made then followed
on inevitably from this and 'cut' for 'coupe' became 'slice' as we

imagined that movement through water and 'reef' became 'rocky shore' as an illustration of the dangers facing the poet and his crew. Michael's title of 'TOAST' needed to become more evocative of that promise made by both poet and Greek warrior to his readers and men and we settled on 'PLEDGE'.

Pledge

Nothing, this foam, pure verse
Referring only to the chalice;
So drowns a far-off troupe
Of sirens, a host of them head first.

We sail on, my motley crew,
With me already lashed to the poop,
While you, luxurious prow,
Slice through winter tides and lightning;

A beautiful intoxication urges me
With no fear of keeling over
To stand and raise a glass

To solitude, rocky shore and star
Or whatever else was worth
Hoisting our white sail for.

A second Odyssean poem we looked at was 'A la nue' from 'HOMMAGE':

A la nue accablante tu
Basse de basalte et de laves
A même les échos esclaves
Par une trompe sans vertu

Quel sépulcral naufrage (tu
Le sais, écume, mais y baves)
Suprême une entre les épaves
Abolit le mât dévêtu

Ou cela que furibond faute
De quelque perdition haute
Tout l'abîme vain éployé

Dans le si blanc cheveu qui traîne
Avarement aura noyé
Le flanc enfant d'une sirène

Michael's first draft of this sonnet was a steady starting point again and we spent quite a few days pushing ideas back and forth before settling upon a final version. Our first draft kept the title of the original French, 'A la nue':

Silenced at the overwhelming
Cloud base of basalt and lava
Not to mention the slavish echoes
By a worthless foghorn

What sepulchral shipwreck (though
You know it, foam, you drivel there)
Supreme against the flotsam
Got rid of the bare masthead

Or concealed what furious for lack
Of any more exalted wreckage
The whole unreal abyss displayed

In a strand of this white a hair
Will out of sheer greed have drowned
The child-like haunches of a siren

The French 'accablante' offered us a sense of 'overwhelmed' and in discussion we moved from 'Silenced' to 'Struck dumb' before settling on 'Dumbstruck' with its *coup de foudre*, lightning-strike of immediacy. The use of the word 'foghorn' for 'trompe' was misplaced we felt: it lacked the seriousness of the original and we played around with the idea of shifting the noun to a verb to give us 'Even to a slavish echo / By a useless trumpeting'. However, this again had a vulgarity to it and we finally settled on 'Nor deceit of a worthless horn'. What we were aiming for was a seriousness which might prompt a reader to be aware of an underlying sense of either an image from the *Song of Roland* or from Browning's 'Child Roland to the Dark Tower Came'. We also decided to change the title from the original opening line of the French to 'Beneath the Skies':

Beneath the Skies

Dumbstruck, near overwhelmed
At the foot of basalt and lava cliff
Not excluding enchanting echoes
Nor deceit of a worthless horn

What sepulchral shipwreck (you
Know it, foam, you drivel there)
Erected against flotsam,
Abolished the bare masthead

Concealing what, furious for lack
Of any further high-grade wreckage,
The whole sham abyss laid out

In one strand of bright white hair
Will have drowned in narrow greed
The haunches of an infant siren.

When we were working on the second chapbook of Bonnefoy translations, which were to appear in 2013, we often moved some distance in the attempt to bring things to light. For instance looking at the first untitled poem in the French poet's volume *Pierre Écrite* we paused at the opening two lines:

Prestige, disais-tu, de notre lampe et des feuillages,
Ces hôtes de nos soirs.

Initially we were looking at the word 'Glamour' to open that first line before finally settling on the noun 'magnet':

The magnet, you said, of our lamp and of the leaves,
These hosts of our evenings.

It was with some considerable pleasure that I received an email from Bonnefoy saying *"The magnet of our lamp" pour traduire le très difficile (et aisément misleading) "prestige", c'est bien trouvé. Hardiesse et fidélité together."* I think that both Michael Grant and I took that statement to be a recognition of "Manifest and not abstract" although, as that Canto of Pound's goes on to recognise, "Shall two know the same in their knowing?"

Meditations on a Bewildering Contact with "Translation"

Meditations on Transformations of Lyrics of Women Troubadors

Norman Weinstein

•   After centuries of theories of translation along with
libraries of translated literary texts, let me be Socratic in insisting
that I absolutely still can't find my moorings as to what "translation"
means. So it will be maintained in this essay quotation-marked,
pock-marked, a fiction, filter, scrim, an Ivesian unanswered question.
There's a freedom in not-knowing how to define "translation,"
and that freedom will be revealed in probing the lyrics of female
troubadours, trobairitz, from 12th and 13th century Southern France,
compositions composed in Occitan (ancient French) and carried
into various transformations of idiomatic English. The trobairitz lend
themselves tantalizingly to a reader ignorant of "translation." All that
can be reliably said after centuries of Medieval scholarship is that
they number perhaps three dozen, and somewhat historically reliable
biographical material is available solely for one, the Comtessa de
Dia. Of male troubadours a far more accurate count can be made:
about 2,500. But everything just uttered might be false. There is
no reliable test yet developed to clarify when male troubadours
assumed female voices, and visa versa. So unless you're prepared
to take Virginia Woolf's position that "anonymous," surely a most
commonplace author, is always a woman, we are left with a gender

ambiguity. That said, the starting place for establishing trobairitz literary legitimacy, and even examples of genius by these possibly first women of secular verse, begins with *Songs of the Women Troubadours* edited and translated by Matilda Tomaryn Bruckner, Laurie Shepard, and Sarah White (Garland Publishing, 1995). This is from their introduction:

> In order to understand and appreciate the accomplishments of these 'trobairitz" . . . we need to situate them and their poems in a variety of contexts, literary and historical, cultural and linguistic.

• What is lost when these four contexts are neglected? The first book to popularize Women troubadours in English was Meg Bolin's *The Women Troubadours*. Bolin, by no means an Occitan scholar, relied often on English translations largely by Frederick Goldin, author of the first popular anthology of male troubadours in English, and additionally utilized Oscar Schultz-Gora's anthology of trobairitz texts in German, *Die Provenzalischen Dichterinnen* (Leipzig, 1888). The state of trobairitz research and translation has come a long way since 1888, but that wasn't not really the point. Bolin's book aligned speculative personalities of women troubadours with First Wave feminism of the 1970s. That attractive reduction of the complexity of trobairitz lyricism continues today. Once a trobairitz persona is invented by a gifted re-imaginer – translators by any definition are not necessarily needed for this transformation – variations on this theme can proliferate generously. Nothing wrong per se in this re-imagining if labeled as such – unless one really cares for the weighing of literary, historical, cultural, and linguistic contexts. And don't you, if you join my ranks of the "translation-challenged?"

• So does factoring out literary, historic, cultural, and linguistic contexts to varying degrees necessarily distinguish a "re-imagining" – or "version" – or Robert Lowell-like "imitations" – from a "translation."? Those claiming not would argue that a translator with such a rigorously narrow definition of "translation" risks a literalism siphoning the poetic spirit, the imaginative leaps shaping original trobairitz composition. But here's an inconvenient truth about existing trobairitz lyrics in English translation: only *Songs of the Women Troubadours* was created by translators knowing Occitan. And here is why that matters.

  • The poet and translator Pierre Joris drew my attention to an absolutely remarkable publication deserving a wide readership, *Grains of Gold: An Anthology of Occitan Literature* (Francis Boutle Publishers, 2015). Edited by the Occitan translator James Thomas, it reveals that Occitan literature that marked its poetic origins in 12th/13th century troubadour and trobairitz lyrics is still a radiantly alive source of first-rate lyric poetry today. No longer can trobairitz poems in Occitan be treated as relics from a dead language that have to be carried forward from German translations into credible idiomatic current English. It is worth knowing Occitan with the seriousness that the poet Paul Blackburn gave to it (years of study with the best scholars from The University of Wisconsin and The University of Toulouse, plus his extended correspondence with Ezra Pound). The magnificent and still unequalled troubadour translations of Paul Blackburn in the recently republished *Proensa* (New York Review Classics, 2016) display a virtuoso sense of word play, a reminder that these were stylized performances for royal courts that nevertheless took delight in status-bumping, surprising twists and turns Eros offered. Here's a closing stanza from Blackburn's translation of Marcabru's *Estornel, cueill ta volada*:

> The disloyalty
> she has done me
> I make it even
> pay her back
> and give myself to her, the devil.
> But under me
> she'll have to be on the level,
> and then hug me
> and then nip me . . .

Read aloud, a mind meld seems to occur between Marcabru and Blackburn, the poem an enactment of a dance of the intellect, a parallel aesthetic two-step in reference to the Feminine in devilish, when not sacred, when not warmly human, form. With an utterly simple vocabulary, note the multiple meanings that common words like "even," "under," and "level" assume. Hear the courtly rhythms that Pound heard in the Occitan of Arnaut Daniel's lyrics that he called "joyful and jazzy" in his *The Spirit of Romance*. And note how the teasing dynamics of the timeless "game of Love" within the conventions of courtly love are played out. Robert Duncan spoke of writing poetry "to exercise his faculties at large." That applies to Blackburn in *Proensa*. Detailed knowledge of the source language of troubadour poetry was synthesized with knowledge of the cultural, historical, and literary backdrop of this literature. Even more. Blackburn's ear for the most colorful erotic banter between modern men and women, his showcase of archetypal New Yorkers of the late 1950s/ 1960s gave his English versions a sense of performative edge and verve. Whatever else might be soundly speculated about male and female troubadours writing in Occitan, they were literary entertainers of the highest order. What does "literary entertainer" imply in our time?

    •   Am I awaiting someone with Blackburn's grasp of the four levels of Occitan medieval troubadour literature – literary, cultural, historic, and linguistic – to bring her talents to trobairitz lyricism? Yes. Am I also longing for idiomatic English translation with the rhythms of courtly dance while simultaneously displaying contemporary American musicality in erotic banter? Yes. Listen to Billie Holiday sing: "The difficult I'll do right now, the impossible after a while." Meantime, here are two examples of the state of trobairitz translation. The first is from the previously mentioned *Songs of the Woman Troubadours*, the second section of a canso, an emotionally direct lyric form in a single voice, the opening stanza, by Comtessa de Dia:

> I must sing of what I'd rather not,
> I'm so angry about him whose friend I am,
> for I love him more than anything;
> mercy and courtliness don't help me
> with him, nor does my beauty, or my rank, or my mind;
> for I am every bit as betrayed and wronged
> as I'd deserve to be if I were ugly.

Here is the version offered by Claudia Keelan in her *Truth of My Songs: Poems of the Trobarairitz* (Omnidawn, 2015):

> I sing of things better left unsaid
> confessing the rage I feel for him
> who I've wanted more than anything.
> All my pity and good girl deeds died,
> along with my body, soul, and brain
> since I've been played the total fool
> and used like some old, useless tool.

To be fair to both versions, a reader should be aware of Keelan's assumptions about who the trobairitz were, and why they composed what they did lyrically. In her book's introduction, Keelan asks "So why translate the poems of 12th century teenagers?" Keelan finds attractive the drama and emotional extremes of adolescence played against the reality that teenagers are often powerless. She links that to their popular music that expresses a full and intensely immediate emotional range. So that a fusion is made with today's teen girls and the trobairitz. As to her view of "translation," she quotes Ezra Pound's "All ages are contemporaries" as a justification of her "translation":

> The trobairitz's concerns are still women's concerns, and
> to carry that across, I listened for contemporary sounds
> in which to make those matters manifest . . . as I began
> translating these poems in 2011, I heard the sound of 12th-
> century pop culture, A Middle Ages version of rap or hip-hop,
> the rebellious music of the young, whose love exists in a
> complex of concerns always personal, and yet indelibly set
> amid a society seen as oppressive . . .

To advance deeper into Keelan's sense of "translation":

> Before translating I first read the Provencal, (NW's note:
> "Provencal is a dialect of Occitan") listening for the
> homophonic connection (most often I would translate the
> Provencal word to an equivalent sounding English word).
> To honor a vernacular that disappeared long ago, I worked

to find approximate English idioms to lend the right tone for their constant oneupsmanship.

• To return to looking at these versions of trobairitz lyricism, look at the contrast between the fourth line of each. In the Bruckner, Shepard, and White version:

mercy and courtliness don't help me

And in Keelan's version:

All my pity in good girl deeds died

Keelan's version removed the Medieval lyric from historic and cultural and religious contexts by replacing "mercy" and "courtliness" – words of extraordinary intellectual and emotional dimensionality in 12th century Southern French courts – with the ordinariness of "pity" and the wryly modern feminist ring of "good girl deeds." Do these displacements make for a strong trobairitz poetry in English? Does the casting of the trobairitz as defiant teenage girls bring across their essence, even assuming the concept of "adolescence," an invented 20th century sociological category had an exact parallel in 12th century Provence society? And how do rap and hip-hop rhythm tracks (both specifically products of the African diaspora – not merely a general "rebellious music of the young") - how do these styles popularly produced for consumption largely by aggressive teen boys of all stripes) enhance trobairitz meaningfulness?

• If I credit Keelan's versions of the trobairitz as "translation," wouldn't I also have to hold the recent "translation" of Dante's *Inferno* by Mary Jo Bang as comparable, say, to Mark Musa's. To do so puts aside Musa's lifetime of work as an enormously sophisticated Italian scholar and translator, and places it on the same level of importance as that of a contemporary American poet, no Dante or Italian authority of note, who imaginatively reframes Dante to sound like this in her version of Canto VIII:

> We kept on until we reached the moats
> That defended the Hotel California. The walls high reaching
> To the horrid roof, seemed made of molten iron.

If you want your Dante transposed in time and space to the vagaries of hip L.A. in the late 20th century, Bang is your Dante "translator." But isn't Bang's pop-culturation and Americanized Dante really more about her than about anything ever known over the centuries about Dante? There's nothing wrong in putting pop culture American meat on your Dante skeleton – but calling it "translation" empties that difficult term of any meaning I can hold.

•　　When Keelan turns this canso by Azalais de Porcairages that opens with an invocation to local brokers whose assistance she seeks in winning her love:

> To God I commend Bel Elgar
> And the city of Orange
> And Gloriet and Casler,
> And the Lords of Provence

into

> I hand over the bank to God
> and the city of blank,
> all those prophets of buy and trade,
> the CEO's of all my days …

I sense the poem is totally Keelan's. And her "city of blank" is no more compelling a presentation of the trobairitz's place geographically and metaphorically than Dante's Florence transfigured into the Hotel California in Bang's Dante. And that is not what I expect from "translation." Some of us, to recall that telling phrase of Charles Olson's, like to savor our poetic roots with the dirt – of history, culture, language - dangling to them still.

Addenda:

The most stunning modernized version of trobairitz lyricism in my experience is found performed on an obscure Italian CD, *Lo Mau d'amor* (Felmay, 2010) by a group called "Trobaititz d'Oc." Italian vocalists with folk and jazz expertise, Valeria Benigni and Paola Lombardo, join forces with jazz baritone saxophonist Claudio Carboni in a charmingly riotous program of ancient trobairitz lyrics and original modern folk/jazz hybrid songs all sung in Occitan. If you are interested in what happens when Occitan poetry to set to rap and hip-hop tracks, listen to "Ma ville est le plus beau park" by a male duet called *The Fabulous Troubadours*, a spin-off from another popular Occitan band given to reggae treatments of Occitan poetry, *Massilia Sound System*. Selections from these three bands can be accessed online. While Keelan writes about her struggle to create compelling contemporary poetry "to honor a vernacular that disappeared long ago," these musicians are dynamic proof that Occitan literary and musical creativity is alive and well.

10 Poems

Che Qianzi

1. Non-Poetry

One sleeps into
the universe.

Tip of the head — blood
mating.

2. Non-Poetry

As the beam light's up this place,
never straying,
we've just drawn water from this well,
washing up the kids,
as if we'd like to eat them — washing kidney beans, radishes,
cabbage.

Have you ever stepped on cut hair?

The focus fades . . . radical river's mottled waves,
like a flock of driven sparrows,
in the turbulent yard.

We've just washed up the kids by the well,
ambushed by the surrounding scorched fields, behind the mountains,
behind the sea.

3. Transparency

A drinking glass. Begins to
love water, shy to start with
becomes bolder, big mouth drinks water,
I don't know either,
big big mouth drinks glasses of water,
so much water, where is it stashed?
And so transparent.

Scrambling before the host of gods,
drink up water, a drinking glass.
Why such thirst?
Why not such thirst?
The more thirst, the more vigorous, sincere, loyal, earnest,
humorless,
big big mouth drinks water. It's like tribute.
Where does the water go? Transparency.

Even if accidently smashed, there's no leak.
   (Yesterday, my aunt in the country killed a goose to treat guests,
blood all over. She said:
"more blood than a murdered man."
   (Big big mouth, drinks a glass of water,
On the table, not as clear as milk,
yet still transparent.

Nudging the glass,
the magnet absorbs the dark horse, absorbing—
never ending night, the donkey in the stable most certainly cannot:
consider it a hotel. "His plaything in spring
in winter," natural hardwood frames,
adorned with dozens of strangers, never dreamed,
of being stashed on shore.

"Our sense of history, as delicate as this photo?"

4. Non-Poetry

We are a rough race,
just a single wife,
long since divorced.

5. Childhood of Flies

Tidy up paws, quivering wings,
fish the fly out of the cup.
Then the whirlpool chases the circle's simple eye.
At last one two green high,
turns into a dragonfly.

On the swaying chains become honeybees.

Living beings achieve the way the sweetness of receiving letters:
lips rolling out jelly sweets with eyes revolving,
"Out of Egypt."

I've tasted the lovely jelly sweets from Egypt.
Is it necessary to cross oceans?
My smashed bronze mirror is from Xian.
In a few drowned years, "This river will dry up,
bridges collapse, three fairies return to their caves."

All owing to — one two green,
they simply row a boat,
bask in the sun (but can't fly).

Everywhere death covers the earth,
on the swaying highway become:
once there was a boy.

6. Non-Poetry

Give me, Mount Lu bread, quite stuffing the library,
so many fistfuls cannot hold
                    a handful of snow,
a female chimp at the fireplace,
touches the flames,
eats cream,
watches the white ape,
out on inspection.

Grand scent like the Yangtze,
brothers stride from north to south,
black and white water drips into
        a golden rooster pitcher.

Give me a deep-rooted bone, repay me with
an ancestral home.
Take away official business.
Virgin boys and girls confess in pairs:
the news carved on a tea-brown fruit stone,
immortals cast swords, build ships, worship, ha-ha-harvard.

7. The Grand Canal

1. Vines of distracting thoughts in the pheasant's tail feathers.
Don't just stop, a circle as round:
as a greening tomb. Mother of the Grand Canal.

2. (Mother of the moment.)

3. Green weeds, the Yangtze of Spring and Autumn drowns the Huai
                                                          of Warring States.
"The Huai must be harnessed."
Agnominal "historians," breathing manual labor, flows down. Flows
                                                          down as follows—
hidden swallow money,
from "The mansions of the Wangs and the Xies,"
greening, the aesthetics of an enervated evening.

4. Going down to Taihu Lake,
water lost to Suzhou people,
Taihu stones stand in the courtyard awaiting orders.
Red lacquered gateway, I hear duty's tread travelling across
                                                          mountains and rivers.

5. Invent some misery, "Why don't you speak up!"
Also worth a few coins. Poor spot,
Uncouth stage props — yet local dialects adore donkeys.

The Dame peddling Qingyi river and lake water, Old Servant grinds
                                                          away;
shadow puppets record the play of spring, Slavey grinds ink.
   (as round as the mother of the moment.)

6. Invent some circle as round as the mother of the moment.

   The Grand Canal stuck with no luck.

*Translators' note: The ancient Grand Canal links Beijing with Hangzhou
in the south. Suzhou, the poet's home town, is a major commercial and
cultural center on the canal situated between Taihu Lake and the Yangtze
River. Taihu Lake is a major source of the bizarrely shaped rocks favored for
classical gardens, for which Suzhou is especially famous.*

8. Like Lotus Root

They will never annihilate you – epigraph

It's that kind of weather,
all slippery with promises,
snuggling close in mud,
soul mates for so long, then entertaining bad designs,
invent — light dawns in the seeds of man,
flowers beckon in the breeze,
held by a face cleansed with tears, shut up within the dark self,
disorder gives way to dominion. Bridging,
they let likeness pass over,
a few sweets floating silk,
fairy slung over the shoulder.
  lotus root in muck happy in others' misfortune, because
        worthless? I'm hardly proud of my guilt,
it's spontaneous.
Cut it.
The bridge, held in such high esteem, collapses:
this slippery pleasing hostility,
can split kisses — can produce good deeds:
the flesh dies, the body is aware,
a gust of wind brushes breasts,
like rabbit ears addicted to angels.
Absolutely.
Break it off—
certain episodes of a certain time:
a cleanly severed couple,
each as if occupying their hill, the other in an exquisite coffin,
let time worry,
pretty good, great-grandfather's old city dripping green public park,
warm up the dark womb
        with a fetus,
breeding in the great dark. Landing on all fours,
thunder rumbles from red lips,
hair like seeping water.
Only fear can return as utter fearlessness.
This year,

an uninvited guest lounges on a rude steel-wire bed,
is there motherhood or an embroidered quilt,
to cover an erect mind?
Sometimes a damp nail dreams through the night,
an ashamed lighthouse emulates a nail
          buried in an unmarked grave.
Leave the slick tide, the chatter,
dodging into madam's embrace, rusts
a conceptual food basket filled with immortal food,
deep thoughts in the courtyard, slip ups,
like masterpieces, and a sticky rice society.
I'd like to pat the ass of a documentary film.
A price war in the market,
a crime committed over face paint, a warning received from
          plant pests,
can only admire
          the soft Suzhou dialect – snowy asses – who loves a slut,
she folds up
          both injured lotus tassel legs,
move over, crrrash, study Soviet roulette abroad,
obediently following the earth's revolutions
          the earliest gamblers were monks and ascetics,
even squeamish swans feed only on toads.
Is it the same where you come from?
Come to the blossom meeting.
   (black lotus root, white lotus root.
Lotus root, snaps into clinging halves,
now colorless,
the name is some kind of nonferrous metal;
a likeness, in the dark womb,
it's that kind of weather so gentle
          tender shoots in the holes, a people
dark womb of the public park,
a panda sleeps.
Since the nation's founding, the privatization of lotus root,
picked clean, a photo in an album of fragrant affairs,
leaving behind the smelly pond,
manroot in life like a fountain pen,
all are classifications and right click dragonflies,

select a similar text format,
stick to the nipples of lotus flowers,
misfortune becomes celebration.
Chains run to relieve the guard, crraash, a lucky rice straw,
leaves an unlucky egg,
      to save it's life.
Merely a river, both longing on Broken Bridge,
still a demon.
Women of the future revisit old haunts,
according to men, unreliable handwriting, and
      the happiness index,
to build a pagoda.
History is not written as a dirty novel, however
      it's a brothel
unable to make its accounts public.
   (the riddle's answer is for sale.
Yet
      lotus root, your cloister swept by a machine gun,
images of sages on the wall with innumerable gaping wounds,
alter the sordid interior: white submarine,
even domesticated animals are unwilling to be left out,
conscience still fondly patrols,
therefore cut it, absolutely, absolutely break off
      the swill.
Lotus root, in your cloister a panda sleeps.

*Translators' note: lotus root, which is commonly eaten across much of Asia,
is a rhizome that grows as a series of linked sausage-shaped tubers, tan-
colored on the outside and white inside, prominently perforated by holes.*

9. Abdomen

Your sufferings are enough
to skin a toad
from the body.

This toad
too is skinned.
It jumps into the clear sky,
steps slowly at the bottom of my well,
a womb drop
human milk.

And the womb, the womb of the she-wolf.

The way circles round the lake without end,
cut off the password,
a lonely islet, hops,
hops to the abdomen.

   (Your sufferings are enough,
to bring up the wedding toast,
from the body.

The she-wolf,
she eats only one bowl of rice.

10. Anomalous Faction

Bitter rose petals . . .

Revision: won't repair — love now.
A perfectly round pie! Snow left on the ground, lives
                    under-cooked,
giving,
alms for the carmine forehead,
an anomaly.

They rotate one after another around the tower,
in the lambs' miserable sucking sound,
stretching to a spell under the belly,
white lane is also (a dream:
put on a black river's sinister arms,
like a just removed jacket.
Bitter rose petals . . .

Bitter, on bitterly decorated roses'
                    beginning — only then:
can rose petals protect.

Blooming is anomalous.

                    — *Translated by* Jenny Chen and Jeffrey Twitchell-Waas

A Diver's Explanation

Che Qianzi

Facing translation, the poet should be a diver deep underwater. The translator floats on the surface.

In the spring of 2015, Jeff visited Jiangnan (south China). We had originally planned to meet in Suzhou, but unfortunately I was busy moving house in Beijing, so I asked my friends Jenny Chen, Li Dewu and Lao He to receive him. Jenny informed me that Jeff was a bit concerned because while in Nanjing he had heard a rumor that I had stopped writing poetry. How could I stop writing poems? I am always writing. This year I prepared four books of poetry for four different publishers, more than 600 poems nearly all new, except for *Selected Poems of Che Qianzi, 1976-2016*, which covers a relatively long period of time. Which is to say, aside from making a living, my entire energy, labor and interest is in writing poetry. Jenny asked me to select some poems to read at a poetry party my friends organized to welcome Jeff, which they then decided to translate.

When Jeff read "Non-Poetry":

| 人睡入 | One sleeps into |
| 宇宙。 | the universe. |

He remarked to Jenny: "I understand Che Qianzi's conception, the contrasting shapes of "人" [one, person] and "入" [go into, agree with] constitute the *dao*, yin and yang emerge in the poem."

I was quite surprised on hearing this, surprised at Jeff's sensitivity to the Chinese written characters. Sensitivity to the characters has formed my conception of poetry — I believe Chinese poetry should start from the written characters, from the poem's shadow:

Written characters, the poem's consumed shadow or perhaps the shadow that refuses to be consumed. Dangerous, keep true to the shadow's reality.

The character of Chinese poetry is determined by the written characters.

The Chinese poet's senses are elsewhere, in other places, in other views, immersed in the seen. Perhaps one might say, written characters act as image writing for those who use Chinese; arriving long ago at an obstinate, taciturn, four-sided stillness, precisely like a picture, from the outset the visual makes its demand. For Chinese poets this demand is especially severe.

Written characters act as image writing, without setting out an argument, or sound reasoning. Its compositional character is not philosophic; under the pictorial sense of the ideas, the depths are poetic thought. The compositional character of written characters is poetic thought; it's quick-witted, that's the first law. Alphabetic writing traverses a flat plane; written characters exist above, in the middle, below, or in all directions (east south west north) — a three-dimensional junction, a convergence point, an entering point and a vanishing point....

The perspective of written characters is unfathomable, certainly it is a dispersing perspective.

There's a covering quality. I also think written characters possess a covering quality, thus safeguarding the weight of the poem's shadow.

Regarding the poem's shadow, weight is quality. Written characters are not merely the appearance of the poem; writing that lacks understanding and respect for the quality of written characters ignores the poetic thought of Chinese poetry.

Just as there is no status in a dictionary, one cannot demand status. Poetic thought has status, written characters do not....

Simply put, poetic thought can be summed up as this type of language thinking. That is, it is the form of the written characters that still retain the language thinking before the formation of the written characters. This point, the comprehension of this point, will release the brilliance of Chinese poetry.

However the achievements of Chinese language poetry are opposed to Chinese language. A distinct expression against the social habits of the Chinese language heightens the achievement of Chinese poetry. Opposition to the written characters, wherein lies imagination and eruptive power, distinguishes the philologist.

The character of Chinese poetry is determined by the written characters, but if Chinese poetry becomes inflexible it will be brittle and shatter at the first blow.

The above extracts are picked from my writings on poetry, by which I still stand:

The shadow silently but surreptitiously changes the completed poem.

Because my poetry writing starts from the written characters, it inevitably creates difficulties for translation, inevitably involving enormous loss. The difficulties are those of the translators, Jeff and Jenny, the losses are mine. Yet I love the losses—without loss there is no poetry. The best home for poetry to return to is translation because nothing creates a greater loss in poetry than translation. In my view this loss is active and creative: the poet offers a musical score, the translator and reader perform it. And the translator is more like a band conductor.

Among this group of translated poems, "Like Lotus Root" is, even for Chinese readers, quite obscure; I have quietly set up puns, allusions, jokes, slogans, advertising tags, folk tales … almost as a practical joke on the translators. If Jeff and Jenny feel that way, that would please me — why can't poetry today be a prank? Yet "Like Lotus Root" is no prank. Compared with this world where danger lurks on all sides, is thoroughly absurd, a practical joke may actually be decent and serious.

Moreover, don't think my writing is Chinese poetry. Among my fellow writers, some use Chinese to write American poems, or French poems, or British poems, or Argentinian poems, or Soviet poems, some use Chinese to write Chinese poems.

I hope my poems — have no nationality. Yet also are not globalized.

I hope my poems — Chinese poems written with characters even when translated into a foreign language without written characters are still Chinese poems.

12-18-2016 Beijing

— *Translated by* Jenny Chen and Jeffrey Twitchell-Waas

Translator's Note

In current internet jargon, "a diver" is a surfer who looks in without participating in chat groups and forums—remaining submerged. However, facing the poem, the translator floats on the surface.

Che Qianzi's supposed surprise at my observation on the visual aspect of certain characters is puzzling, given that he has ceaselessly spoken to this point ever since we first met 25 years ago. However, this, as with much of the autobiographical framing of his remarks ought to be taken as Che Qianzi's characteristic mischievous fabling, mixed with the considerable deflections in our communications due to the mutual limitations of our capabilities in each other's language.

Given the limitations of my Chinese, I have always worked with a collaborator and over time have developed a regular, if rather laborious routine. I ask Jenny to translate the poems quite literally, noting any ambiguities, word play, shifts of register, allusions and the like. I then work through the Chinese text with this preliminary translation making copious notes and questions, some of which may be directed to the poet. This process goes back and forth through at least five or six versions until we have worked our way into sufficient familiarity with the poem and seem to have an acceptable rendition in English. At which point it is put aside for at least a few months and then returned to with fresh eyes and ears. That is the unglamorous yet always edifying process. If I act as the final arbiter, Jenny mediates every detail.

More due to my linguistic limitations than translation theory, my propensity is to mimic the syntax of the Chinese poem or prose without unduly tampering with the abrupt looseness that has sometimes been taken from a Orientalist perspective as the Chinese language's agrammatical character, even more pronounced in classical Chinese which continues to assert its presence in most modern poetry. In the case of Che Qianzi at least this seems justified for reasons indicated in his remarks above.

— Jeffrey Twitchell-Waas

Metal City

Joaquín Borges Triana
(Robert Arellano, tr.)

I'd just gotten home a few hours from a trip to German Democratic Republic, and after I told a few stories to mom and dad and the beloved employees at my workplace, **Alma Mater** magazine, I got the call to hit the road again, off to Santa Clara by invitation from Hermanos Saíz Association, sponsors of Cuba's first rock festival known from this day forward as **Metal City**. I pulled into the capital of Villa Clara and the welcome offered by a planner was to say with dour enunciation that he could provide no accommodation although I'd confirmed participation with two months advance notification!

Lucky for me I've got a long connection with a couple who hold me in their affection and offered up their house for me to sleep in and to make my breakfast, lunch, and dinner, thus the hostess holds me in such favor, she who detests all culinary labor. —For certain, it's a shame I must admit how logistically this festival fit the definition of CHAOS, near-TOTAL, without pointing blame at the promoters, who did much more than should be their ration, but that for a lack of integration across the diverse organizations called upon for such a celebration.

Among the outrages at Metal City were: audio problems (eternally); performance starts (unpunctually); suspension of scheduled activities; inadequate hospitality (the musicians' first two nights accommodations were certainly magnificent locations for falling victim to all kinds of mites and still larger insects who love bites!); but most of all the complete nonexistence of someone to control the undisciplineds who climbed the stage in Liberation Theater obstructing bands with blundering behavior.

This litany of mishaps notwithstanding, it's an important step we are ascending on a stairway we must climb to hasten letting **metal** into the family of our nation. Burden whom it might burden, this musical language has for two generations of youth been the common sonic tongue.

Three days and nights Santa Clara swarmed with creatures of every size and form arriving from the island's furthest corners two thousand on average for each line up of performers. There were those who looked on with surprise or with frank rejection at the people passing by—watch them take the city by wildfire, lighting up the streets with their wild attire! But over and above their eccentricity the central region's rockers show a high degree of intelligence, as is the case of Ernesto Pulido and Javier Leyva, who wildly enjoyed days of events and musicianship each band presents.

The quality of groupings was most impressing; Gens, for one, well deserves recognition for their many years as firm supporters of a genre that, wisely played, endures, a set list in which they mixed heavy with the **hard** from the different stages of their repertoire; although they continue within metal song, beside the latest trends, their sound remains strong.

It was very pleasing to see the debut of Estirpe, a group with antecedent in another renamed Cenit, and they proved that, if adequately programmed, and they work hard, they deserve to be included in the island's **heavy** metal scene. Once again, Zeus showed how they're imbricated in the rock of **thrash metal**: orchestrated pieces with constant timing changes. This band sounds better and better every day, and the only thing lacking which I find a pity is a lead singer that would give more possibility for Luiso, the group's current vocalist, to loosen up his prowess in his other role as lead guitarist.

Sentencia's members are others who shred it; the second they hit the boards, I give them credit: for sheer power of sound and a great stage presence, they capture the audience; among rockers of our nation, this quintet is playing with most energy transmission. At last, there was Alto Mando who, for me, most connect, a virtuoso band that emerged among Cuba's **heavy metal** elect. They won the prize for best songwriting, which, in conjunction with the event, I was judging, and I can assure you the remaining lyrics submitted were also of notable merit.

I will mention, although it be tangential, that Metal City undertook a theoretical panel in which intervened a group of experts; moreover, there were giveaways of posters, and allegorical pullovers for sale. All of this was made possible by Communist Youth, the likes of Rosita and Bofill. Furthermore, there were envoys of Radio Progreso, Opina, and of television programs *En Confianza* and *A Capella*. And I wish to specially recognize Roger and Veitía of Asociación Hermanos Saíz, two who, with no vocation whatsoever as organizers, made possible this dream that promises to become a reality next summer again. But you won't have to wait that long for another festival, for according to reports of unofficial information obtained from my friend Luchi, whose station is in the Amateur Rock Musicians Association, August will see scheduled two meetings of this same nature in the capital, Havana.

Finally, as with my generation hundreds of Cuban boys and girls like to rock, struggling for a future that is better, not by any small victory over misunderstanding and prejudice, fighting for their right to grow up under the influence of a music that at last has begun to pulsate in the concert halls, shaken to their foundations — let metal into the family of our nation!

Translator's Note

Robert Arellano

I was at the Rockefeller Foundation Bellagio Center this recent autumn, working on a nonfiction book about *Los Frikis*, a name embraced by the most extreme death-metal music fans in Cuba. Three decades ago, some of them entered a pact in which as many as 200 of them deliberately self-injected HIV-positive blood. Within a few years, most of them had died of AIDS (this was years before Cuba had access to antiretroviral drugs), but there are a few survivors who trace the origin of the *Friki* resistance to a three-day music festival, the first such event ever permitted by the Cuban government, which would also be, for an entire decade following, the last.

The only review that exists of the concert was published in Cuba by a Young Communist Union magazine. While translating it for my book, I was struck how this review on the face of it, is a hack job. There are very few details of the show, as if the reporter merely needed to prove to his editor that he actually attended the event. There is barely if any actual review of a concert here. One solipsism followed by another, the language sounds stereotypically, socialistically stilted to capitalist ears, but somehow still manages to surprise. What other country could produce rock concert reporting like this:

"I will mention, although it be tangential, that Metal City undertook a theoretical panel in which intervened a group of experts; moreover, there were giveaways of posters, and allegorical pullovers for sale."

What rock journalist would note the presence of "allegorical pullovers"? Ultimately, this is a very close, almost literal translation (including the boldface formatting of the original publication), but I labored over identifying rhymes when I could, and if you broke down my columns you would find that practically every paragraph is a self-contained stanza in iambic pentameter with an AABB rhyme scheme. (I actually worked with this in verse form for most of the translation process, and it was a last-draft decision to return the stanzas to narrow-column paragraph formatting like the original.)

"Just as a tangent touches a circle lightly and at but one point, establishing, with th s touch rather than with the point, the law according to which it is to continue on its straight path to infinity, a translation touches the original lightly and only at the infinitely small point of the sense, thereupon pursuing its own course according to the laws of fidelity in the freedom of linguistic flux." – W. Benjamin

"The One that could repeat":
On Translating Susan Howe's
My Emily Dickinson

Antoine Cazé

"As a great poet, Dickinson possessed the chameleon-capacity to change color in mid-stanza by the manipulation of a word, even one letter." (93)[1]

"Chameleon"—wonderful word for "Translator." Mediator of sameness and difference. Passing for someone/thing else; passing through several milieus, several landscapes of language—this word a world, rocky pebbly way—, and mutating colors, slightly off if one looks closely enough, at some sub-word pigmentary level. Survival technique to deceive predators. But what if Predator turns out to be Chameleon. "I can add colours to the chameleon"—Richard III in his famous "dissembler" monologue (III, ii), quoted by Susan Howe. By her account, Dickinson's poem of the frontier—"My Life had stood – a Loaded Gun –"—ventriloquizes Shakespeare, HER gun HIS dagger: "I can smile, and murder while I smile" (Richard)/"And do I smile ... None stir the second time." (Gun) Translator (ME/MY) to ventiloquize Howe channeling Dickinson writing through entire libraries. Can the translator out-chameleon the chameleon?

---

[1]All page numbers in brackets refer to Susan Howe, *My Emily Dickinson*, NY, New Directions, 2007 (first published in 1986).

(Never King though, never Richard Heart of Lion; but coming IIIrd, and illegitimately, doomed to grovel—Gk χαμαιλέων: Lion on the Ground.)

Chameleon is a transparent word, for an English-French translator. Chameleon IS *Caméléon*. Or is it? One letter is missing/Une seule lettre vous manque… What's in a letter: H, SH, SHe, SHakespeare, S(usan) H(owe). Add a letter here, subtract one there. Commenting on another animal—the doe that does appear in Dickinson's poem—, Howe notes how its final letter "e" somewhat mischievously appears in some old spellings of the verb "do." Examples in Shakespeare and John Donne. In *Bottom: On Shakespeare*, Louis Zukofsky calls that kind of attention to the letter, "eyeing intimacies of print," which he says are "all action, as tho 'a soul feminine saluteth us'" (104, quoting Zuk quoting Shakespeare's *Love's Labours Lost*). Paying attention to the physicality of writing brings out the feminine inside. A final "e" is the common mark of the feminine in French.

And now We hunt the *Doe* –

    And *do* I smile,

        Our good Day *done* –

Unlike English, French is a gender-inflected language. Grammar be confusing. Possession a chiasmus of genders: English identifies Owner when French identifies Owned: possessives keep changing *ma/mon ta/ton sa/son* regardless of possessor. "Change shape with Proteus"—Richard again. Hiding her colors. Wait! HIS colors. Colours. Say it in French! "Cachant SES couleurs."

Will Chameleon kill Doe in the masquerade of translation? How ironic is it that this final feminine "e," linking doe and do, proved to be one of the residual untranslatables in (my) French. How, Susan? I had to make do(e) with a footnote, a bullet shot right in the h(e)art of this feminine/masculine trans-action. Can this doe ever smile again, in French?

An H and an E. HE. H(ow)E. The feminine hurts—kills, even.

Howe can I be "her"? Pass for Her, She? The one the two who says who say MY from the very first word of her book/her poem? Howe can *My Emily Dickinson* become "My" Emily Dickinson in "my" language? MON langage/MA langue. "Mon" Emily Dickinson in the words of another.

> Possession – in translation –

> Be Tricky Transaction –

"My voice formed from my life belongs to no one else." (13). As a male translator, I still speak with *MA voix* of *MA vie*, in the feminine. To what extent does such a blurring ungender/engender/endanger MA translation? Which has to be written in her voice with my words. Formed from. The FORM of possession depends on the language from which you look at it. It's a matter of (gender) orientation—the FROM of possession. Can't have it both ways. Or can I? Translation as cross-dressing, queering the text; some things must remain at odds in a translated book. This book (*my life I read it first 30 years ago*) begs me to write "Odd secrets of the line."[2]

My *Emily Dickinson*	*Mon* Emily Dickinson
My *Life had stood*	*Ma* Vie passa

Parallel lost. Adjust paradoxes. MON a "false masculine" here, merely required by the vowel that follows it—phonetics superseding grammar. MON is MA in disguise: in a momentary flash of her English reflected on *mon français*, I truly own Emily Dickinson. Or she owns me. Not unlike HE being *contained* in SHE: "How do I, choosing messages from the code of others in order to participate in the universal theme of Language, pull SHE from all the myriad symbols and sightings of HE." (17-18)

(Bonus: *Mon* visually rhymes with *Dickinson*, Son of Richard, Sun of York. *Ma* actually does rhyme with *passa*.)

The main thrust of Howe's argument for reading Dickinson is about blurring gender lines. Howe doing it, Dickinson doeing it. Frontiering Gender, not gendering the frontier— roaming, pioneer, knight errant, estray.

---

[2] "Therefore, as One returned, I feel/Odd secrets of the line to tell!" Emily Dickinson, F132/J160 (1860).

ESTRAY]   *sb. Law.* 'Any beast not wild, found within any Lordship, and not owned by any man" (Cowell) 1594.

        adj. That is astray (*rare*)

Roaming the woods of two languages, on this moving frontier line that no fool in a dark tower can decide to close to the necessary foreignness of our common human condition, Childe Translator remains an estray—a vagrant, a migrant.[3] "Not owned by any man."

Childe, another mute "e" added to change meanings. Howe's title for Part Two: "Childe Emily to the Dark Tower Came" (31). From a French perspective, Childe has a feminine ending. Was Susan Howe consciously unmanning her Child? Choosing not choosing gender. But in French, Childe as Attendant to a knight must be gendered: Écuyer/Écuyère. Changing colors by the manipulation of one letter to dislocate masculine and feminine:

ChildE Emily to the Dark Tower Came

À la tour noire est parvenuE l'Écuyer Emily.

Subject is masculine but verb be feminine. Action is in the Doe. "Acquiescence in hunting herself—archaic Doe in sovreign was her own free action." (104)

This Doe cannot be a Poetess. Poetesses are Victorian sissies. Not this one who wrote "She dealt her pretty words like Blades" (F458/J479, 1862). The Poet/Gun can doe; has the willpower for virile action. Howe deconstructs rigidly binary feminist readings of Dickinson the better to reveal the masculine power coiled inside the feminine. "[A]nd when I try to organize – my little Force explodes – and leaves me bare and charred – I think your called me 'Wayward'." Said Dickinson to Thomas Wentworth Higginson (August 1862). GUN is a SHE, Loaded and Lethal. Firing back, she explodes with glee:

> And do I smile, such cordial light
> Upon the Valley glow –
> It is as a Vesuvian face
> Had let it's pleasure through –

---

[3]Solely referring here to Browning's "Childe Roland to the Dark Tower Came": "The round squat tower, blind as the fool's heart"—a centerpiece in Howe's reading of Dickinson.

Dickinson sets out to unman power. By taking her Gun Poem apart for over a hundred pages, Howe unravels the power game she sees at play in Dickinson.

When she first wrote to Thomas Wentworth Higginson, April 1862— asking him, in the mock suppliant tone she liked to put on, if her Verse was "alive"—, Emily Dickinson addressed him pointedly as "Mr. Higginson." Mister/Master. Coyly pretending to consent to the normalizing of gender he had performed at the outset of the "Letter to a Young Contributor" she was responding to: "My dear young gentleman or young lady,—for many are the Cecil Dreemes of literature who superscribe their offered manuscripts with very masculine names in very feminine handwriting…"[4]

"Superscribe" vs. Underwrite: This is a serious game of power to know who actually *signs* a poem, or a letter. Or a translation. GUN be PEN. Who will have the upper hand? "The power to kill" or "The power to die"?

"Mr. Higginson, Are you too deeply occupied to say if my Verse is alive?"
Pretty blade, dealt pretty sharply.

Should it be "Lettre à un jeune contributeur," then, or "Lettre à une jeune contributrice"? How can I blur these gender colors, the way Richard dissembles to kill? The way Susan Howe makes Gun into Wife into Woman? The way Dickinson plays Dickindaughter to Higginson?

Essaying to translate Howe's essay has dislocated me from the comfort zone of clear roles. "A Day," Howe's text passed, "identified/ And carried Me away –" from my dusty corner, forcing me to perceive that yes even in French, Fusil could not only be Woman, but Feminine Word, and all the stronger for being thus *désaccordée*. I learned how to make words *disagree* with each other: "Après

---

[4]Thomas Wentworth Higginson, "Letter to a Young Contributor," *The Atlantic Monthly*, Vol. IX, April 1862. *Cecil Dreeme* is a gothic novel by Theodore Winthrop (1861), an early example of queering gender in American letters. To be fair, it must be acknowledged that Higginson was a staunch champion of women's (and slaves') rights throughout his life, as Howe explains and explores at length.

une journée bien remplie passée à écrire sous l'inspiration de son Maître, *le poète, seule*, dans sa clairière du Devenir, continue à expérimenter."

SHE, "wandering through zones of tropes" (18), taught me to experiment, to repeat with a difference. Translators are taught not to repeat: it's frowned upon—called *calque*, loan translation. Chameleon/Caméléon. Repeating *fait mauvais genre* in translation. Wrong gender, too. In her poem "The One that could repeat the Summer Day," Dickinson challenges this indeterminate, genderless "One" to be a He when trying to repeat an essentially feminine experience, translate its color:

> The One that could repeat the Summer Day –
> Were greater than Itself – though He –
> Minutest of Mankind – should be –
>
> And He – could reproduce the Sun –
> At Period of Going down –
> The Lingering – and the Stain – I mean –
>
> When Orient have been outgrown –
> And Occident – become Unknown –
> His Name – remain –
>
> (F549/J307, 1863)

SHE dares HIM to remain a SON and be able to reproduce this SUN in HER Period—and at "Going down" (sunset), the word does "mean" *that* red Stain, too. Challenging creative powers of (re) production.

> If you saw a bullet hit a Bird – and he told you he wasn't shot – You might weep at his courtesy, but you would certainly doubt his word. One drop more from the gash that stains your Daisy's bosom – then would you *believe*?...[5]

Without the power to die. Translation. Transaction. Transgender. Is Childe Translator's Name meant to remain?

---

[5]Dickinson's second so-called "Master letter" (1861) out of the three she wrote to an unknown recipient, but never sent.

Qui Pourrait Répéter

(a related poem)

Antoine Cazé

I

Ma	*My*
Langue	Debout
Stood	Siffle
Chargée	Glaciale
Blows	Sureau
Elder	*Loaded*
Icy	Cette
Cygne	*Tongue*
Calcine	Scalpe
Cette	Force
Force	*Swans*
Scalps	Passèrent
Poésie	*Charred*
Propriétaire	Dessus
Passed	Frigide
Over	*Poetry*

Frigid	Hisse
Perle	Sans
Hoisted	*Owner*
Sans	*Pearl*

Sortie	*Exits*
Hésite	*Exist*

II

Vie	*Life*
Ma	Évanouie
Frigide	Cette
Vacille	Glaciale

Vanished	Vue
Dessus	*Out*
This	Sapin
Sight	*Frigid*

Sans	*Vacillate*
Icy	*Hesitate*
Fir	*Over*
Hissé	Vésuve

Stood	Saigne
Cerveau	Épris
Hésitant	*Hoisted*
Breuvage	Signe

Swoon	Debout
Vesuvius	*My*
Swan	*Beverage*
Taken	*Brain*

Locks	Coagule
Clots	Prise

III

Demeure	*Stood*
Ma	Signal
Vie	*Out*
Fusil	*Bled*
Fanal	*My*
Signal	Vitre
Fatal	Hisse
Saignée	Autour
Frigide	*Life*
Pane	*Fatal*
Sans	Scintille
Éprise	*Beacon*
Scalped	Vésuve
Crise	*Frigid*
Around	Sortit
Sparkles	Scalp
Or	*Crisis*
Hoisted	*Taken*
Sortit	Fusil
Vesuvius	*Gold*
Éclat	*Death*
Mort	*Bright*

IV

Là	*Had*
Demeure	Laisse
Ma	Neige
Vie	Lèvres

Lips   Contre
Out   *My*
Clots   *Stood*
Hiver   Travers

Laisse   Cygne
Cygne   Calciné
Through   *Life*
Snow   Sans

Gun   Cerveau
Vésuve   Winter
Against   Coagulé
Vitre   *Scalping*

Éclate   Neige
Brain   *Vesuvius*
Scalpe   *Bright*
Charred   Fusil

Bite   Brillante
Bright   Morsure

V

Gun   Fusil
Demeure   Sans
Là   Sureau
Ma   Abreuve

Vie   *My*
Out   Passante
Perle   Frigide
Crise   *Stood*

Floods   Contre
Vésuve   *Crisis*

Cheveu	*Had*
Signé	Poésie
Frigid	*Pearl*
Calcine	Morte
Elder	Éclate
Passing	*Signed*
Poetry	Hair
Against	*Vivid*
Bright	*Chars*
Death	*Vesuvius*
Sûre	*Owned*
Propriétaire	*Sure*

VI

Loaded	Chargé
Demeure	Là
Had	*Gun*
Ma	*Stood*
Life	*My*
Fusil	Vie
Blessée	Encercle
Souveraine	Cette
This	*Wound*
Rigide	Froide
Colder	*Sovereign*
Circles	*Rigidity*
Dead	*Burst*
Éclat	Mort
Death	*Burns*
Éclate	Morte

Mourir	*Burnished*
Écarlate	*Deaden*
Mourut	*Burnish*
Écartelât	*Deadened*

Mort	*Do*
Doe	Mors
Mord	*Did*
Died	More
Morts	*Done*

Mon Emily Dickinson, by Susan Howe, with a preface by Eliot Weinberger, translated by Antoine Cazé. To be published May 2017, Paris, Ypsilon Éditeur.

Notes on Contributors

Robert Arellano is the author of six novels including the online hypertext *Sunshine '69* and the Edgar Award-shortlisted *Havana Lunar: A Cuban Noir*. His next book, *Havana Libre,* is forthcoming in December from Akashic Books. He teaches in the emerging media and creative writing programs of the Oregon Center for the Arts at Southern Oregon University.

Andrea Augé is an artist and art director for film/video and print living in Seattle.

After nearly forty years of school-teaching **Ian Brinton** now writes full time. Recent publications include an edition of *Selected Poems and Prose of John Riley* (Shearsman), translations from the French of Philippe Jaccottet (Oystercatcher Press), *For the Future*, a *festschrift for J.H. Prynne* (Shearsman), *An Andrew Crozier Reader* (Carcanet) and *Contemporary Poetry and Poets since 1990* (C.U.P.). He co-edits *Tears in the Fence* and *SNOW* and is involved with the Modern Poetry Archive at the University of Cambridge. He is the Web Manager for The English Association's War Poets Website.

Antoine Cazé is Professor of American Literature and Literary Translation at University Paris Diderot. He wrote his PhD dissertation on Emily Dickinson and is a board member of the Emily Dickinson International Society. He is the author of a monograph on John Ashbery, a book-length study of H.D.'s Trilogy, and some 60 articles on American poetry (among which three on Susan Howe) published in scholarly journals. He has translated many American writers into French, including contributions to the recent collective retranslations of the works of F.S. Fitzgerald and Jack London for Gallimard/La Pléiade.

Che Qianzi (original name Gu Pan) was born in 1963 in Suzhou, China and now lives in Beijing. He has published more than 30 books of poetry, essays and paintings, most recently *Serious*, *Papaya Play* and *Lao Che: Idle Paintings*. Regarding himself, "The self in one's poetry is mere artwork," no more than that. Among various further translations into English of his poetry is *Vegetarian Hugging a Rooster* (Barque Press, 2002) and selections in *The Big Red Book of Modern Chinese Literature*, edited by Yunte Huang (Norton, 2016).

Jenny Chen (Chen Yajuan) was born in 1964 in Suzhou, China, where she continues to live, and is a graduate of Suzhou University.

George Economou is the author of fifteen books of poetry and translations, the most recent of which are *Unfinished & Uncollected: Finishing Cavafy's Unfinished Poems and Uncollected Poems and Translations* (Shearsman Books, 2015), *Complete Plus—The Poems of C. P. Cavafy in English* (Shearsman Books, 2013), *Ananios of Kleitor* (Shearsman Books, 2009), and *Acts of Love, Ancient Greek Poetry from Aphrodite's Garden* (Modern Library of Random House, 2006). He hopes to spend the next few months working on a book of more "Exercises in Rough Trade."

Alec Finlay: (1966–) Scottish poet, publisher and artist. He has published over thirty books; recent publications include *a-ga* (2014), *A Company of Mountains* (2013), and *Today Today Today* (2013), *ebban an' flowan* (2015), *a better tale to tell* (2015), and *Global Oracle* (2014). His work crosses over a range of media and forms, from poetry, sculpture and collage, to audio-visual and new technology.

Much of Finlay's work considers how we as a culture, or cultures, relate to landscape. Finlay blogs regularly at http://alecfinlayblog. blogspot.co.uk

Jesse Glass' pioneering erasure poetry series *Man's Wows* (Chax Press) was featured in *Wiederaufgelegt; Zur Appropriation von Textern und Buchern in Buchern (Lettre Transcript)*, Anette Gilbert, ed. in a chapter on Appropriation and Conceptual Writing. His series of photograph/poems is available at the *Peacock Journal* site, and will appear in the *Peacock Journal Anthology*. *A Charm for Survivors, Selected Painted Books and Sequences* is available from The Knives Forks and Spoons Press, and is volume one of several projected volumes. *Anguipede*, a collection of poetry, is at press, and the *Complete Gaha Noas Zorge* is also in production, while continuing to darkly flower.

Peter Hughes is a Cambridge-based poet who is a member of the European Union. He runs Oystercatcher Press. He teaches creative writing at Cambridge University where he is the current Judith E. Wilson Visiting Poetry Fellow, and a Fellow of Magdalene College. His hobbies include walking upstream, tinkering with old Italians and wondering if there's time to learn German. His sensitive yet twangy versions of Petrarch's sonnets came out from Reality Street in 2015. His Cavalcanti comes out from Carcanet in May 2017.

Hank Lazer has published twenty-four books of poetry, including *Poems Hidden in Plain View* (2016, in English and in French), *Brush Mind: At Hand* (2016), *N24* (2014) and *N18* (2012), *Portions* (2009), *The New Spirit* (2005), *Elegies & Vacations* (2004), and *Days* (2002). *Selected Poems and Essays of Hank Lazer*, completed by a group of translators, was published by Central China Normal University Press in 2015. Lazer's Selected Poems have also been published in Italy and will be appearing shortly in Cuba (including 11 tracks for jazz-poetry improvisations with soprano saxophonist Andrew Raffo Dewar). Readings and interviews can be accessed through PennSound: http://writing.upenn.edu/pennsound/x/Lazer.html , as well as in special issues of *Plume #34* and *Talisman #42*. In 2015, Lazer received Alabama's most prestigious literary prize, the Harper Lee Award, for lifetime achievement in literature. His books of criticism include *Opposing Poetries* (two volumes, 1996) and *Lyric & Spirit: Selected Essays 1996-2008* (2008). With Charles Bernstein, he edits the Modern and Contemporary Poetics Series for the University of Alabama Press. Lazer retired from the University of Alabama in January 2014 from his positions as Associate Provost for Academic Affairs, Executive Director of Creative Campus, and Professor of English.

Robert Mittenthal is author of *Wax World* (Chax, 2011), and a variety of chapbooks including: *Value Unmapped, Martyr Economy, Ready Terms,* and *Irrational Dude.* He was instrumental in creating and curating the Subtext Reading Series (1995-2009) in Seattle, and the last few years has been working to induce collective thought via a series of related reading groupuscules, a project called: autonomous university. He blogs at http://rmutts.blogspot.com/

Toby Olson's eleventh novel, *Walking,* will appear soon from Chatwin Press. Currently, he's writing short stories and poems.

Paul Pines grew up in Brooklyn around the corner from Ebbets Field and passed the early 60s on the Lower East Side of New York. He shipped out as a Merchant Seaman, spending part of 65/66 in Vietnam, after which he drove a cab until opening his Bowery jazz club The Tin Palace, the setting for his novel, *The Tin Angel. Redemption*, a second novel, is set against the genocide of Guatemalan Mayans. *My Brother's Madness*, a memoir, explores the unfolding of intertwined lives. He has published thirteen books of poetry: most recently *Message From The Memoirist* and *Charlotte Songs.* He lives with wife, Carol, in Glens Falls, NY, where he practices as a psychotherapist and hosts the Lake George Jazz Weekend. His website: paulpines.com

Joe Ashby Porter has completed the novel *Forgotten Coast*, two chapters of which appeared in GHR.

Ariel Resnikoff's most recent works include the collaborative pamphlet, *Ten-Four: Poems, Translations, Variations* (Operating System, 2015) with Jerome Rothenberg, & the chapbook, *Between Shades* (Materialist Press, 2014). New poems, translations & critical prose, can be found/are forthcoming in *Jacket2, White Wall Review, karawa, Mantis & Dibur* journal. With Stephen Ross, he is translating into English Mikhl Likht's Yiddish modernist long poem, 'Processions', & with Lilach Lachman & Gabriel Levin, the collected Hebrew writings of Avoth Yeshurun. Ariel teaches creative w/reading at the Center for Programs in Contemporary Writing (UPenn) & curates the "Multilingual Poetics" reading/talk series at Kelly Writers House.

Jeffrey Twitchell-Waas lives in Malta and edits the Z-site on the works of Louis Zukofsky (www.z-site.net).

Norman Weinstein's six books of poetry include one entitled *Weaving Fire from Water*, a title he's taken seriously lately by learning to weave on frame looms, inspired by Anni Albers' weaving books and classes at Black Mountain College as much as he's been inspired by Black Mountain poets. Other threads he's followed resulted in *A Night in Tunisia: Imaginings of Africa in Jazz, Carlos Santana: A Biography,* and a book on Gertrude Stein's writing. He teaches Educational Philosophy as well as Canadian Studies at Boise State University. And resides in Boise, Idaho, with his beloved wife Mary.

Lightning Source UK Ltd.
Milton Keynes UK
UKOW01f1836040917
308576UK00004B/10/P